WHO NEEDS TO OPEN THE CAPITAL ACCOUNT?

Olivier Jeanne, Arvind Subramanian, and John Williamson

Peterson Institute for International Economics
Washington, DC
April 2012

FSC
www.fsc.org
MIX
Paper from
responsible source
FSC® C00501

D0962740

Olivier Jeanne has been senior fellow at the Peterson Institute for International Economics since 2008. He is a professor of economics at the Johns Hopkins University and has taught at the University of California Berkeley (1997) and Princeton University (2005–06). He is a research affiliate at the National Bureau of Economic Research (NBER), Cambridge, MA, and a research fellow at the Center for Economic Policy Research, London. From 1998 to 2008 he held various positions in the Research Department of the International Monetary Fund. He has served on the editorial boards of several journals, including the *Journal of International Economics* and *International Journal of Central Banking*.

Arvind Subramanian is senior fellow jointly at the Peterson Institute for International Economics and the Center for Global Development. He is the author of *Eclipse: Living in the Shadow of China's Economic Dominance* (2011). *Foreign Policy* magazine named him as one of the world's top 100 global thinkers in 2011. He was assistant director in the Research Department of the International Monetary Fund, served at the GATT (1988–92) during the Uruguay Round of trade negotiations, and taught at Harvard University's Kennedy School of Government (1999–2000) and at Johns Hopkins' School for Advanced International Studies (2008–10). He advises the Indian government in different capacities, including as a member of the Finance Minister's Expert Group on the G-20.

John Williamson, senior fellow, has been associated with the Institute since 1981. He was project director for the UN High-Level Panel on Financing for Development (the Zedillo Report) in 2001; on leave as chief economist for South Asia at the World Bank during 1996–99; economics professor at Pontifícia Universidade Católica do Rio de Janeiro (1978–81), University of Warwick (1970–77), Massachusetts Institute of Technology (1967, 1980), University of York (1963–68), and Princeton University (1962–63); adviser to the International Monetary Fund (1972–74); and economic consultant to the UK Treasury (1968–70). He is author, coauthor, editor, or coeditor of numerous studies on international monetary and development issues, including *Reference Rates and the International Monetary System* (2007), and *Curbing the Boom-Bust Cycle: Stabilizing Capital Flows to Emerging Markets* (2005).

PETER G. PETERSON INSTITUTE FOR INTERNATIONAL ECONOMICS
1750 Massachusetts Avenue, NW
Washington, DC 20036-1903
(202) 328-9000   FAX: (202) 659-3225
www.piie.com

C. Fred Bergsten, *Director*
Edward A. Tureen, *Director of Publications, Marketing, and Web Development*

Typesetting by Susann Luetjen
Printing by Versa Press, Inc.
Cover design by Peggy Archambault
Cover photos: © Fotolia

Printed in the United States of America
14   13   12   5   4   3   2   1

Library of Congress Cataloging-in-Publication Data
Jeanne, Olivier.
  Who needs to open the capital account / [Olivier Jeanne, Arvind Subramanian, John Williamson].
      p. cm.
  Includes bibliographical references and index.
  ISBN 978-0-88132-511-9
  1. Capital movements. 2. Capital. 3. Capital—Accounting. 4. Investments, Foreign. I. Subramanian, Arvind. II. Williamson, John, 1937–III. Title.
  HG3891.J43 2012
  332'.0424—dc23

                                    2012003377

Contents

Tables

Figures

Box

Preface

Although economists generally agree that countries can derive substantial gains from international economic integration, the extent to which they should open themselves to international capital flows remains a controversial issue. The Peterson Institute's research and publications over the years have reflected the diversity of views on the benefits of globalization, but never by following the fashion of the day. In his book *Has Globalization Gone Too Far?* (1997) Dani Rodrik presented a skeptical view of globalization at a time (before the Southeast Asian crisis) of widespread optimism about the benefits of capital flows to emerging-market and developing economies. More recently, William Cline's *Financial Globalization, Economic Growth, and the Crisis of 2007–09* (2010) reaffirms that financial globalization represents a significant factor in economic growth of emerging-market economies, at a time when many have second thoughts about the benefits of financial liberalization.

In this book, Senior Fellows Olivier Jeanne, Arvind Subramanian, and John Williamson revisit the question of how developing and emerging-market economies should integrate into global financial markets. There is still, 20 years after the rise of emerging-market finance, a wide diversity of approaches to capital account policies. Some emerging-market economies maintain a completely open capital account. Others, most notably Brazil, have experimented more actively with market-based prudential capital controls since the crisis. And still other countries, such as China, maintain tight restrictions on their capital accounts.

Jeanne, Subramanian, and Williamson argue that this diversity of policies is consistent with the lack of strong evidence for or against the benefits of capital account liberalization. They show—using a "meta-regression" approach incorporating a large number of empirical specifications—that free capital mobility seems to have little impact on economic development (although there is some evidence that foreign direct investment and stock market liberalization may, at least temporarily, raise growth). Furthermore, economists now understand better the welfare benefits of prudential capital controls of the type that Brazil is using to curb the boom-bust cycle in capital flows. The question of capital controls is a technical, not an ideological, one: Some controls may be appropriate under certain circumstances, whereas others may be harmful. Accordingly, there is no rationale for the international community to promote totally free trade in assets—even over the long run.

This being said, Jeanne, Subramanian, and Williamson find the status quo—in which there is no international rule or discipline for capital account policies—problematic. On the one hand, the lack of commonly agreed rules implies that capital controls are still marked by a certain stigma, so that the appropriate policies may be pursued with less than optimal vigor. On the other hand, certain capital account policies may have harmful multilateral effects and negative spillovers on the global economy. This is particularly the case of policies that repress domestic demand and, through a combination of reserve accumulation and restrictions on inflows, maintain a current account surplus. Those policies have the same economic effects as trade protectionism and undermine the global public good that is free trade. Thus, Jeanne, Subramanian, and Williamson see a need for an international regime that would legitimize the use of capital account policies that are appropriate and discourage the use of those that are not.

The book concludes by proposing the desirable features of an international norm for capital account policies. As for trade in goods, if there are controls, Jeanne, Subramanian, and Williamson would be strongly in favor of having transparent, price-based measures, such as a countercyclical tax on certain types of capital flows. The international community could agree on a ceiling on the tax rate to ensure that the harmful effects of controls (if any) would be limited. The new rules could be embodied in an international code of good practices developed under the auspices of the International Monetary Fund.

The Peter G. Peterson Institute for International Economics is a private, nonprofit institution for the study and discussion of international economic policy. Its purpose is to analyze important issues in that area and to develop and communicate practical new approaches for dealing with them. The Institute is completely nonpartisan.

The Institute is funded by a highly diversified group of philanthropic foundations, private corporations, and interested individuals. About 35 percent of the Institute's resources in our latest fiscal year were provided by contributors outside the United States. The Ford Foundation provided generous support for this study.

The Institute's Board of Directors bears overall responsibilities for the Institute and gives general guidance and approval to its research program, including the identification of topics that are likely to become important over the medium run (one to three years) and that should be addressed by the Institute. The director, working closely with the staff and outside Advisory Committee, is responsible for the development of particular projects and makes the final decision to publish an individual study.

The Institute hopes that its studies and other activities will contribute to building a stronger foundation for international economic policy around the world. We invite readers of these publications to let us know how they think we can best accomplish this objective.

C. FRED BERGSTEN
Director
March 2012

Acknowledgments

We are grateful to Dani Rodrik and Anton Korinek for insightful discussions on financial globalization and to Kue Peng for valuable research assistance.

deficits that could jeopardize macroeconomic stability or to prevent overvaluation of a currency that would excessively weaken the tradable goods sector.

Bad controls distort capital flows in harmful ways. The most onerous capital account restrictions, both before and after the start of the global financial crisis, are those used by countries such as China to competitively prevent the appreciation of their currencies, thus distorting international trade and capital flows. The role of capital account restrictions in distorting the real exchange rate is broadly understood, but its central importance is not. As we argue in this book, accumulating international reserves would be much less effective in preventing real currency appreciation in the medium to long run if such accumulation were not supplemented by severe restrictions on capital inflows. In the case of China, the government induces "forced saving" in the domestic private sector in order to finance the current account surplus, which in turn contributes to prolonging global imbalances and lowering employment in the rest of the world.

The second main conclusion of this book is that it would be desirable for a code of good practices concerning capital account policies to be developed under the auspices of the IMF.

The first reason for such a code is that, under some circumstances, unconstrained national actions can be collectively damaging.[5] A second reason is that such a code would reduce the stigma associated with capital controls: The current lack of rules stigmatizes countries for not following whatever happens to be the conventional wisdom at the time, which in recent years has favored free capital mobility. As a result, countries that have recently imposed capital controls have often done so apologetically and with less-than-optimal vigor. Finally, a code would help define a set of best practices that countries can aim for in implementing capital controls.

But we also argue that the "rules of the road" for managing capital flows should go even further. Any set of rules will fail to address the biggest challenge posed by capital controls if it is limited to blessing the controls that are deemed to be appropriate but fails to discourage the use of restrictions that are harmful. Any code of good practices for capital controls that is developed should also be used to define by exclusion controls that are presumed to be distortive and should not be used.

Looking forward, the presence of distortive capital controls raises an issue of deep concern: the asymmetry between the existence of a strong multilateral framework for international trade in goods and the absence of rules for trade in assets. The WTO and its predecessor, the General Agreement on Tariffs and Trade (GATT), promulgated strong rules to promote free trade in goods. In contrast, trade in assets has been left largely to the discretion of individual countries, reflected most saliently in the fact that the IMF has no jurisdiction

---

5. For example, if all countries held their capital at home with no change in the ultimate pattern of investment, investors would be deprived of the benefits that attend the lower risk exposure of holding more diversified portfolios.

over its members' capital account policies. This asymmetry makes no sense because, as outlined in this book, capital account policies (including the accumulation of reserves) can be used to achieve exactly the same trade effects as tariffs on imports and subsidies for exports. Thus, any conflict about international trade has a natural tendency to spill over to capital flows, and vice versa.[6]

This asymmetry between trade in goods and trade in assets will become increasingly problematic for the global economic system. It was not a fundamental problem under the Bretton Woods system (when capital account restrictions were widespread) because global trade integration was much less advanced than it is today and exchange rates were managed multilaterally. Nor was it a serious issue when global trade integration involved primarily advanced economies, because these economies were simultaneously opening themselves to international capital flows. Finally, it was not perceived to be a pressing problem before the Great Recession, when the global economy was close to full employment (even though growth was being achieved at the cost of large imbalances that were already becoming a concern). But looking forward, several factors—including especially a persistent global demand deficit and the rising share of China in world trade—will lay bare the inconsistency of having multilateral rules and institutions for trade in goods and no multilateral framework for trade in assets.

What should be covered in a code of good practices for capital account policies? This is not an easy question: The difference between "good" and "bad" capital controls resists easy definition. There are many species of capital controls. Capital controls can cover inflows or outflows. They can be administrative or market based.[7] They can be prudential—aimed at reducing the risk of financial instability—or used for other objectives, such as limiting the appreciation of the domestic currency.[8] They can be implemented anticycli-

---

6. For example, consider the proposal that the United States respond to China's accumulation of dollar reserves by "countervailing interventions" (C. Fred Bergsten, "We Can Fight Fire with Fire on the Renminbi," *Financial Times,* October 4, 2010). This strategy is motivated by the desire to address a trade imbalance, but it is difficult, if not impossible, to implement in practice because of the heavy restrictions on the Chinese assets that US authorities could buy. There is no treaty or framework by which the international community can compel China to sell more of its domestic assets to nonresidents.

7. Akira et al. (2000, 7) define administrative (or direct) capital controls as controls that "restrict capital transactions...through outright prohibitions, explicit quantitative limits, or an approval procedure," whereas market-based (or indirect) controls "discourage capital movements and the associated transactions by making them more costly to undertake." Another (related but not identical) distinction is between price-based and quantity-based controls. Price-based controls take the form of a tax on capital flows and are also market based. We would also classify quantity-based controls as market based if they take the form of tradable quotas. The important criterion in determining whether a control is market based is whether the induced price distortion is observable in a market.

8. In some cases, limiting the appreciation of the currency may itself have a prudential motivation (as discussed in chapter 2).

cally to counter booms and busts in capital flows, or they can be structural. This book makes the case for one type of capital control that we consider to be important—price-based, prudential, and anticyclical controls on inflows—but this does not mean that all appropriate controls must have those features. For example, a country may want to protect a fragile banking system with administrative structural controls, at least for a while.

Establishing international criteria to distinguish the good varieties and uses of capital controls from the bad ones is a difficult but not an impossible task, and the stakes justify that it be tried. What should be the basic principles? We discuss in the conclusion to this book various options that presume different degrees of international coordination and multilateralism. Our most ambitious proposal can be summarized as follows:

- The international community should not seek to promote totally free trade in assets—even over the long run—because (as we show in this book) free capital mobility seems to have little benefit in terms of long-run growth and because there is a good case to be made for prudential and other nondistortive capital controls. But, as for trade in goods, if there are controls, we would be strongly in favor of having transparent, price-based measures. We recognize that the judgment call about what level of controls is appropriate in a given circumstance may be difficult in practice and propose that the effective tax implied by market-based capital controls should not exceed 15 percent (a level consistent with the recent literature on the optimal taxation of capital flows).

- Administrative (non-market-based) controls may be justified in some cases, but the primary justification for them should be prudential—that is, to promote or preserve financial stability. The IMF should develop the jurisprudence to define the appropriate circumstances and measures.

- The new rules could be embodied in an international code of good practices developed under the auspices of the IMF. Because the framework of international trade rules would then encompass both goods and assets, the new regime should be accompanied by a system for institutional cooperation between the IMF and the WTO, as proposed by Aaditya Mattoo and Arvind Subramanian (2008).

The interdependence of international trade in goods and international trade in assets underlies the argument for increased international oversight of capital account policies. In particular, one impetus for the 15 percent threshold is to limit real exchange rate distortions and thus to help maintain a level playing field for international trade.[9] From this point of view, our proposal is comparable to others put forward to limit exchange rate misalignments. Some of these other proposals target norms for such variables as exchange rates or

---

9. Under some conditions, the impact of capital controls on the real exchange rate is of the same magnitude as a tax on capital flows (see chapter 2).

current account balances, but the economic justification for such norms is often debatable.[10] Other proposals focus instead on the policy instruments that underlie the distortions (such as foreign exchange intervention or, as we do here, capital account policies), which has the advantage of avoiding the need for strictly defining the desirable outcomes.

The global financial crisis generated a multilateral response, but the impetus for global cooperation created by the crisis has weakened, and that may leave little hope of achieving international agreement on far-reaching, global financial reforms. In particular, what would be the incentives for those who regard themselves as potential losers, such as China, to participate in such an agreement? There is a menu of options—including both carrots and sticks—available to induce cooperation, as discussed in the conclusion. Using the example of China, the carrots could take the form, in the area of trade in goods, of granting China the status of a market economy, and in the area of trade in assets, of securing investment opportunities for its sovereign wealth funds. The sticks could take the form of restrictions on exports, restrictions on foreign asset holdings, or taxation of the yield on foreign assets of countries that fail to abide by the new rules (Gagnon and Hufbauer 2011).

The book is structured as follows. Chapter 1 reviews the experience of developing and emerging-market economies with capital flow volatility during the global financial crisis and discusses the resurgence of controls on capital inflows, with special emphasis on Brazil. Chapter 2 presents the case for prudential capital controls, but then argues that existing controls are often not prudential in nature and instead appear aimed at maintaining a persistent currency undervaluation. Chapter 3 revisits the question of whether capital account liberalization has a significant impact on growth using a "meta-regression" approach that measures the robustness of the results across a large number of empirical specifications. Chapter 4 looks at the same question but focuses on certain types of capital flows (equity, foreign direct investment, and bank flows) and their likely microeconomic consequences. Finally, the last chapter takes stock of the analysis and presents our main policy conclusions.

---

10. In particular, they require making an implicit judgment about the appropriate saving and investment rates for given countries.

Capital Flows to Developing and Emerging-Market Economies during the 2007–10 Crisis

This chapter reviews the behavior of capital flows to developing and emerging-market economies during the 2007–10 crisis (table 1.1 lists the economies included, by region). The volatility observed in the fall of 2008 was unprecedented in size and scope, but it was not qualitatively very different from the volatility observed during earlier sudden stops in international capital flows. In particular, as during previous episodes, bank loans and portfolio flows tended to be more volatile than other types of capital flows. One feature that does distinguish the 2007–10 crisis is that it spurred more widespread use of capital controls as a tool for the prudential management of capital flows rather than as a tool solely for crisis management. The main example is the introduction of controls on capital inflows by Brazil, which is reviewed in detail at the end of this chapter.

Capital Flow Volatility

Figure 1.1 shows a measure of capital flows to and from developing and emerging-market economies between the first quarter of 2007 and the third quarter of 2010. Four types of flows are reported as a percentage of aggregate GDP: foreign direct investment (FDI), bank loans, portfolio flows (equity and bond), and other flows excluding banks. The figure also reports the accumulation of foreign exchange reserves on the side of outflows.

There was a sharp, sudden stop in capital inflows in the last quarter of 2008, just after the failure of Lehman Brothers Holdings Inc., when the volume of gross inflows fell from about 8 percent of GDP to about −10 percent of GDP.[1] The sudden stop reflected mainly the reversal in bank loans and port-

---

1. The inflows are reported as gross rather than net flows in the sense that they are not reduced by

Table 1.1 Developing and emerging-market economies, by region

Region	Economies
Latin America and the Caribbean (28)	Argentina, Belize, Bolivia, Brazil, Chile, Colombia, Costa Rica, Dominica, Dominican Republic, Ecuador, El Salvador, Grenada, Guatemala, Guyana, Haiti, Honduras, Jamaica, Mexico, Nicaragua, Panama, Paraguay, Peru, St. Kitts and Nevis, St. Lucia, St. Vincent, Suriname, Uruguay, and Venezuela
East Asia (17)	Cambodia, China, Fiji, Indonesia, Kiribati, Laos, Malaysia, Mongolia, Myanmar, Papua New Guinea, Philippines, Samoa, Solomon Islands, Thailand, Tonga, Vanuatu, and Vietnam
South Asia (8)	Afghanistan, Bangladesh, Bhutan, India, Maldives, Nepal, Pakistan, and Sri Lanka
Europe and Central Asia (21)	Albania, Armenia, Azerbaijan, Belarus, Bosnia and Herzegovina, Bulgaria, Georgia, Kazakhstan, Kyrgyzstan, Latvia, Lithuania, Macedonia, Moldova, Poland, Romania, Russia, Serbia, Tajikistan, Turkey, Turkmenistan, and Ukraine
Middle East and North Africa (12)	Algeria, Djibouti, Egypt, Iran, Iraq, Jordan, Lebanon, Libya, Morocco, Syria, Tunisia, and Yemen
Sub-Saharan Africa (45)	Angola, Benin, Botswana, Burkina Faso, Burundi, Cameroon, Cape Verde, Central African Republic, Chad, Comoros, Republic of Congo, Côte d'Ivoire, Eritrea, Ethiopia, Gabon, Gambia, Ghana, Guinea, Guinea-Bissau, Kenya, Lesotho, Liberia, Madagascar, Malawi, Mali, Mauritania, Mauritius, Mozambique, Namibia, Niger, Nigeria, Rwanda, Senegal, Seychelles, Sierra Leone, Somalia, South Africa, Sudan, Swaziland, São Tomé and Principe, Tanzania, Togo, Uganda, Zambia, and Zimbabwe

Note: Table 1.2 does not include data on Afghanistan, Bhutan, Vietnam, and Somalia.

Source: International Monetary Fund.

folio flows, and it was relatively short-lived: Capital inflows returned to their precrisis level by the third quarter of 2009, less than a year later. However, the composition of the inflows had changed: Bank inflows remained close to zero while portfolio flows rebounded—a change that probably reflects the persistent risk aversion of advanced-economy banks after the failure of Lehman. Strikingly, however, FDI remained stable, even as other inflows were highly volatile.

---

the capital outflows generated by residents (which are reported in the second panel of the figure), but they are net of the asset sales by nonresident investors. A negative number indicates that foreign investors sold more domestic assets than they purchased during the quarter.

Figure 1.1   Capital flows to emerging-market economies (excluding China), 2007Q1–10Q3

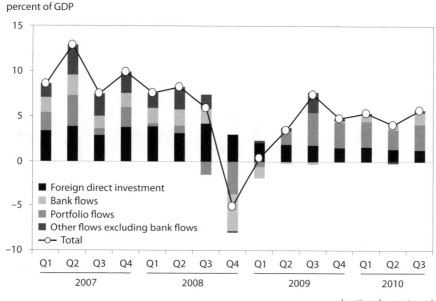

a. Gross inflows

(continued on next page)

The second panel of the figure shows how gross capital outflows from developing and emerging-market economies behaved before, during, and after the crisis. Foreign exchange reserves are both the largest and the most volatile component. These economies were accumulating reserves at rate of 5 percent of GDP per year in 2007, but their stock of reserves declined by almost 10 percent of GDP during the post-Lehman sudden stop. By the end of 2009, however, these economies were again accumulating reserves at the same pace as before the crisis.

The experience of developing and emerging-market economies with capital flows around the time of the Lehman crisis can be summarized as follows. In the fall of 2008, there were very large outflows of bank and portfolio flows, the impact of which on the current account and domestic demand was largely buffered by an equivalent reduction in the stock of reserves, which mitigated the repercussions of the sudden stop on the real economy.

Was the 2008 sudden stop unusual? Figure 1.2 shows the same capital flows a decade earlier, starting at the time of the Asian financial crisis (1997–98) and continuing through the subsequent crises in Russia (1998) and Brazil (1998–99). There are several similarities between the crises of the 1990s and the recent crisis. First, the reversal in gross capital inflows in both cases involved

Figure 1.1   Capital flows to emerging-market economies (excluding China), 2007Q1–10Q3 *(continued)*

b. Gross outflows

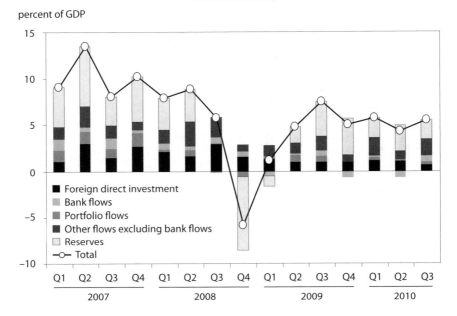

Notes: Includes 27 emerging-market economies: Argentina, Brazil, Bulgaria, Chile, Côte d'Ivoire, Dominican Republic, Ecuador, Egypt, El Salvador, Hungary, India, Indonesia, Korea, Malaysia, Mexico, Morocco, Pakistan, Panama, Peru, Philippines, Russia, South Africa, Thailand, Tunisia, Turkey, Uruguay, and Venezuela. Quarterly data are unavailable for China.

Source: International Monetary Fund, Balance of Payments (BOP) database.

mostly bank and portfolio flows, whereas FDI was relatively stable. Second, the impact of the reversal on net capital flows (or the current account balance) was largely buffered by a decline in international reserves.

There were also some differences between the two periods. First, the magnitude of both inflows and outflows was larger during the recent crisis. Bank and portfolio gross inflows fell to almost –8 percent of GDP in the fall of 2008, whereas they never fell below –4 percent in the 1990s. However, this partly reflects the fact that the 2008 sudden stop was caused by a common shock at the center of the global financial system and therefore hit a large number of countries at the same time, whereas the previous crises were less synchronous. The crises of the 1990s took the form of contagion between dominos that fell one after the other at the periphery (first in Southeast Asia, then Korea, Russia, and Brazil).

Overall, however, from the point of view of individual developing and emerging-market economies, there was not a huge qualitative difference between

Figure 1.2 Capital flows to emerging-market economies (excluding China), 1996Q1–99Q4

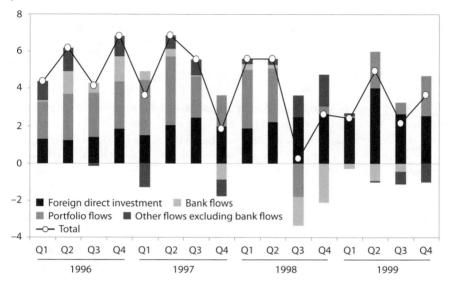

a. Gross inflows

percent of GDP

Foreign direct investment ■ Bank flows ■ Portfolio flows ■ Other flows excluding bank flows —○— Total

1996   1997   1998   1999

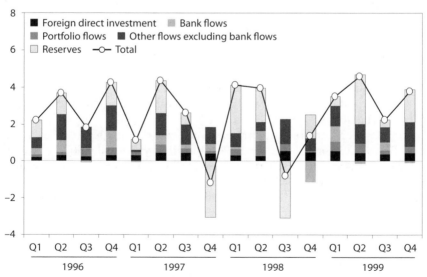

b. Gross outflows

percent of GDP

Foreign direct investment ■ Bank flows ■ Portfolio flows ■ Other flows excluding bank flows □ Reserves —○— Total

1996   1997   1998   1999

Note: See figure 1.1 for list of countries included.

Source: International Monetary Fund, Balance of Payments (BOP) database.

the magnitude of the shock and the types of capital flows involved in the sudden stops of the 1990s and the recent crisis. For example, bank and portfolio gross flows to emerging Asia fell to −13 percent of GDP during the last quarter of 1997 and the first quarter of 1998, compared with −16.5 percent in the last quarter of 2008.

This is not to say that the recent crisis was not novel in other ways—in particular, the collapse of capital flows between advanced economies was unprecedented (see Milesi-Ferretti and Tille 2011). But for most developing and emerging-market economies, the recent crisis was neither the watershed event it was for advanced economies nor as disruptive as the international financial crises of the 1990s.

The pattern of capital flow volatility observed during the 2008 crisis—in particular, the fact that bank and portfolio flows were much more volatile than FDI—is also consistent with the long-run behavior of capital flows during both crisis and noncrisis times. Table 1.2 shows relevant statistics on the flow of four types of capital to all developing economies by region. The first column shows the standard deviation of changes in the net flows to each region, with the change measured relative to the exponential increase in total flows to the region.[2] The remaining columns highlight the relative stability of bank flows versus other flows. The second column shows average net flows, which would be an indicator of stability if the standard deviation were small relative to the average flow. However, the average net flows are negative in a number of instances, an indication that outflows of that category dominated inflows. A more natural way to judge the stability of a particular type of flow is whether its standard deviation is small relative to the average inflow or outflow, i.e., relative to the average *absolute* net flow.

These absolute net flows appear in the third column. The next three columns show the share of the standard deviation of a particular type of capital flow in relation to the standard deviation of the total flow to each region and calculate average flows on both bases to the total flow to the region. The final column includes our preferred measure of the relative variability of different types of capital flow, which is calculated by dividing the figure in the fourth column by the figure in the sixth column.

For all regions, the relative variability is by far the smallest for FDI, then for portfolio equity and for other types of capital, and it is by far the largest for flows of bank capital (more than 13 times as volatile as FDI). These results confirm the conventional wisdom, except that perhaps there was no strong expectation about the relative volatility of other flows. The ordering is similar

---

2. That is, an exponential trend was fitted to total flows to each region, and the size of the regional inflow accounted for by each type of capital flow (FDI, portfolio equity, banks, and other) was deflated by the expected value of the total inflow to the region during that period according to the exponential trend. The standard deviations of these series were calculated.

for most of the regional flows, excluding the Middle East and North Africa (MENA).[3]

For the other five regions, the results are similar except that portfolio equity is more volatile than other flows for South Asia and Sub-Saharan Africa, and other flows are more volatile than bank flows for Europe and Central Asia (ECA). For every region, however, FDI is dramatically less volatile than all other types of flows, and for every region except ECA, bank capital is the most volatile type of flow.

Resurgence of Capital Controls on Inflows

The fact that developing and emerging-market economies have resorted to capital controls is another difference between the recent crisis and the previous crises. The capital controls that were perhaps the most emblematic (and debated) during the late 1990s were measures introduced by Malaysia in September 1998.[4] These were controls on capital outflows whose main purpose was to mitigate capital flight from Malaysia and forestall depreciation of the ringgit. Capital controls, in this case, were used as a crisis-management tool.

By contrast, the recent crisis spurred a revival of the use of capital controls as a tool for preventing crises, not only for managing them. This began in late 2009, when controls on inflows were introduced to deal with a new tide of capital flows from advanced to developing and emerging-market economies. A number of these economies had used such capital controls in the past, including Brazil, Chile, and Colombia during the 1990s, but their use had largely fallen out of fashion[5] (although capital account restrictions were kept in place by some countries including China, which tightly controls both inflows and outflows).

Brazil led the way, introducing a 2 percent tax on all capital inflows except direct investment in October 2009. The rate was increased to 6 percent in October 2010 for bond finance, and the tax was extended to cover derivatives. (The Brazilian experience is described in more detail at the end of this chapter.)

Several other emerging-market economies also introduced controls on capital inflows during 2009 and 2010. In November 2009 Taiwan introduced a ban on capital inflows for time deposits. In June 2010 South Korea introduced curbs on capital inflows. The measures introduced by Korea's central bank had three major components: restrictions on currency derivative trades; enhanced restrictions on the provision of bank loans in foreign currency; and further tightening of the existing regulations on the foreign currency liquidity ratio

---

3. No such calculations were performed for MENA because it transpired that the predicted flow was approximately zero and deflating by zero gives an undefined number.

4. The Malaysian controls have been studied by a number of authors including Kaplan and Rodrik (2002) and Johnson et al. (2007).

5. Chile was phasing out its own system of controls on capital inflows (the *encaje*) during the same month Malaysia was introducing its controls on capital outflows.

Table 1.2 Comparative volatility of different types of capital flows to emerging-market economies, by region, 1970–2010

Flow	Computed standard deviation (deviation from trend)	Average net flows (millions of US dollars)	Average absolute value of net flows (millions of US dollars)	Share in standard deviation	Share in average net flows	Share in average absolute value of net flows	Relative volatility
Latin America and the Caribbean							
Total flows	1.50	27,525	32,812	1.00	1.00	1.00	1.00
FDI	0.33	26,139	26,171	0.22	0.95	0.80	0.27
Equity flows	0.24	3,309	5,669	0.16	0.12	0.17	0.91
Bank flows	0.62	381	5,338	0.42	0.01	0.16	2.56
Other flows	0.97	−2,062	14,436	0.65	−0.07	0.44	1.47
East Asia							
Total flows	2.37	35,452	38,541	1.00	1.00	1.00	1.00
FDI	0.54	38,223	38,223	0.23	1.08	0.99	0.23
Equity flows	0.20	4,541	5,847	0.09	0.13	0.15	0.56
Bank flows	1.24	234	10,403	0.53	0.01	0.27	1.95
Other flows	2.15	−4,207	20,461	0.91	−0.12	0.53	1.71
South Asia							
Total flows	0.55	15,634	15,634	1.00	1.00	1.00	1.00
FDI	0.10	4,135	4,136	0.18	0.26	0.26	0.70
Equity flows	0.39	4,694	5,725	0.70	0.30	0.37	1.92
Bank flows	0.20	1,353	1,871	0.36	0.09	0.12	3.02
Other flows	0.37	6,104	6,830	0.66	0.39	0.44	1.51

Sub-Saharan Africa							
Total flows	2.88	2,406	6,664	1.00	1.00	1.00	1.00
FDI	1.08	5,489	5,522	0.38	2.28	0.83	0.45
Equity flows	1.14	561	2,146	0.40	0.23	0.32	1.23
Bank flows	0.96	−295	1,749	0.34	−0.12	0.26	1.28
Other flows	2.25	−3,349	5,626	0.78	−1.39	0.84	0.93
Europe and Central Asia							
Total flows	1.97	17,276	22,906	1.00	1.00	1.00	1.00
FDI	0.28	14,858	14,858	0.14	0.86	0.65	0.22
Equity flows	0.15	1,517	2,584	0.08	0.09	0.11	0.67
Bank flows	1.00	4,185	10,024	0.51	0.24	0.44	1.16
Other flows	1.28	−1,562	9,926	0.65	−0.09	0.43	1.50
All regions (including Middle East and North Africa)							
Total flows	1.69	96,031	96,574	1.00	1.00	1.00	1.00
FDI	0.29	86,524	86,540	0.17	0.90	0.90	0.19
Equity flows	0.17	11,481	16,168	0.10	0.12	0.17	0.62
Bank flows	0.74	6,049	16,587	0.44	0.06	0.17	2.56
Other flows	1.12	−8,023	37,153	0.66	−0.08	0.38	1.72

FDI = foreign direct investment

Notes: See table 1.1 for the countries included in each region; Afghanistan, Bhutan, Vietnam, and Somalia are excluded from this table. Net outflows (the negative of net inflows) are defined as assets + liabilities (where the International Monetary Fund has omitted the terms indicating changes in assets and liabilities for convenience). Bank flows are taken from the subcategory "other investment," which is a subgroup of the financial account. Other flows are defined as nonresident financial account not included elsewhere less nonresident FDI, nonresident portfolio equity, and nonresident banks. Other flows include debt, derivatives, deposits, loans, and trade credits.

Source: International Monetary Fund, *International Financial Statistics* database, July 2011.

of domestic banks. The currency forward and derivative positions of Korean banks and branches of foreign banks were limited to 50 percent of their equity capital. Indonesia introduced similar but more modest measures during this period, mainly through a one-month minimum holding period on a local-currency debt instrument issued by the central bank (known as Sertifikat Bank Indonesia, or SBIs). In October 2010, Thailand removed an exemption for foreigners on a 15 percent tax on income earned on domestic bonds, and similarly Korea reintroduced a 14 percent withholding tax on foreign investors' earnings from government bonds.

There are several important questions related to the use of such controls, especially the economic rationale and the most appropriate circumstances. But before we address these questions, here is a more detailed review of Brazil's recent experience with capital controls, which provides deeper background for the subsequent analysis.

Case Study: Brazilian Capital Controls

As noted, Brazil introduced a tax on capital inflows in October 2009. The tax rate was initially 1.5 percent but was raised to 2 percent almost immediately. The tax applied to all capital inflows except direct investment. This was feasible because all purchases of *reais* on the official market must be registered with the authorities, and capital inflows therefore can be distinguished from current account and FDI transactions. Because the tax was not proportional to the length of time foreign investors held Brazilian assets, the implicit tax rate was modest on long-term assets held for a long period of time and on short-term assets repeatedly rolled over, but was stiff on very short-term asset holdings.

A straightforward tax on capital inflows is arguably the best form of capital control (e.g., Zee 1999, Williamson 2000), because it creates disincentives for foreigners to invest in the country and incentives for them to hold onto any assets they do buy for a substantial period of time (which was seen as a virtue of the Chilean controls of the 1990s), and because it is simple to implement. Furthermore, there is evidence that inflows of portfolio investment accelerate the growth rate, but there is no similar evidence of the beneficial effect of increased fixed-interest borrowing. This was presumably the reason that the Brazilian authorities raised the tax rate on inflows of fixed-interest capital to 6 percent in October 2010, while leaving the tax rate on inflows of portfolio equity at 2 percent.

Were the Controls Effective?

One disadvantage of capital controls is that they may leave the authorities with the illusion that they have a greater ability to determine the course of events than they actually do. Based on a visit in August 2010, the Brazilian authorities did not suffer from this illusion: They had the impression that investors were complying with the tax, rather than evading or avoiding it, because the tax rate was low. At that time, the SELIC rate[6] was 10.75 percent, compared with the Federal Reserve's discount rate of about 0.2 percent, which made it quite beneficial to hold short-term Brazilian rather than US assets. It was this interest differential, at more than 10 percent, that was motivating capital inflows, and was only reduced to 8 percent by the initial 2 percent capital inflow tax and then only if the Brazilian assets were held for no more than a year; the reduction was more modest if the assets were held longer than a year. Even after the tax rate was increased to 6 percent, there remained a strong incentive for inward arbitrage.

The Brazilian authorities could have had two motivations for instituting this tax: fiscal concerns (namely, to raise revenue) and exchange rate concerns (namely, to limit appreciation of the *real*). Those who consider fiscal concerns to be the primary motivation point out that the tax was introduced shortly after the National Congress of Brazil failed to renew a financial transaction tax that had been in place since 1999. Whether this was the main reason for imposing the capital controls or not, the tax is proving quite successful in raising revenue: The figure mentioned in August 2010 was 0.1 percent of GDP.

The other possible motivation was to limit the strengthening of the *real*. Shortly after the imposition of the tax, the exchange rate abruptly halted what had been a strong appreciation. Between the start of 2007 and the summer of 2008, before the failure of Lehman, the *real* had strengthened from R$2.13 to under R$1.6 per US dollar. In contrast, after imposition of the tax and until October 2010, the *real* hardly exceeded R$1.7 per US dollar.

Because the interest differential remained in excess of 4 percent per year, a flow view of the capital account would predict continuing capital flows into Brazil and therefore continuing appreciation. The more recent stock theory of the capital account draws a somewhat different picture: A change such as the imposition or increase of a tax on capital inflows (or, before that, the sudden stop of capital after the failure of Lehman) would cause a redisposition of capital and, as a consequence, a one-time change in the exchange rate. Under this view, the appreciation before the tax was imposed was a natural reaction to the dissipation of Lehman-induced fears, with the exchange rate perhaps on its way back to its previous level (about R$1.6 per US dollar). Imposition of the tax interrupted this process by reducing the expected excess return on Brazilian assets (that is, the interest differential) as already explained, and therefore reduced the value of the *real* at which a typical investor would balance the added return on Brazilian assets against the danger of a rapid depreciation of the *real* to or beyond its medium-term equilibrium.[7]

However, the *real* again appreciated in 2010, reaching beyond R$1.6 per US dollar in October, and this led the authorities to increase the capital inflow

---

6. The Sistema Especial de Liquidação e Custodia, or Special Clearance and Escrow System, is operated by the Brazilian central bank. The SELIC rate is the central bank's overnight rate.

7. This theory seems to contradict the view that the exchange rate is driven in large part by the expectation that any exchange rate trend is likely to be maintained.

tax on debt finance to 6 percent. The appreciation resumed until mid-2011 but seemed to have stopped by the fall of 2011, though whether or not this is due to the effectiveness of the capital inflow tax is impossible to determine.

Ways to Avoid or Evade the Tax

Critics of the use of capital controls to influence the exchange rate generally point to the problem of preventing tax evasion or avoidance. This has not been much of a problem in Brazil as of August 2010, according to both critics and supporters of the capital inflow tax, primarily because the effective tax rate was so low. There had been inquiries about potential legal ways to avoid the tax, but there were no reports of anyone who had taken such action. A 2 percent tax rate is too low to take the trouble to avoid it.

Given that the exchange rate is widely considered somewhat overvalued, the authorities had room to implement stricter capital controls (that is, a higher tax) from the outset, as they eventually did. What might have deterred them was the fear that a higher tax would have made it worthwhile for market operators to avoid or evade the tax, which would have diminished their ability to prevent an appreciation of the exchange rate and would have eroded the tax receipts.

One form of avoiding the control is paramount. This is for an external investor to arrange with a Brazilian financial institution that it will receive the return earned by a Brazilian investment in return for making an external investment (less a commission) but to leave it to the Brazilian financial institution to purchase internally the equity or debt that earns the return and to hold an external asset. If the Brazilian financial institution wishes to avoid holding an enlarged open position, then it has to buy *reais* for dollars in the exchange market, in which case it adds as much pressure to the foreign exchange market as if the foreigner had invested directly. From the microeconomic perspective of the foreign investor, the operation provides a good substitute for a foreign purchase of Brazilian equity or debt.

There are several additional methods for avoiding or evading capital controls that also limit the effectiveness of the capital controls in influencing the exchange rate. These are much more likely to prove profitable to investors facing higher tax rates on the purchase of *reais*.

The first involves current account transactions. Even systems involving rigid capital controls fail to suppress leads and lags in shifting money over the exchanges. When capital controls create pressure to shift money in, exporters can be expected to repatriate their money more quickly and importers to delay making payments. But even when the traders undertake transactions with foreign investors, the sums that can be shifted in are finite, and a change in incentives would only involve a delay in the movement of capital. Such a delay gives the authorities time to contemplate whether a change of policy is called for. There may also be scope for legitimate market participants to erroneously report the size of their transactions. For example, an exporter might exaggerate the value of foreign sales in order to bring in through the official market foreign capital in addition to actual earnings. Or an importer might understate the cost of foreign purchases, allow a foreigner who desired to purchase a Brazilian asset to make up the difference, and subsequently buy the asset and transfer it to the foreign investor. The potential size of any such "leakage" is limited by the ability of the authorities to estimate the true value of a given volume of exports or the true cost of a given volume of imports, and this ability is distinctly greater for commodities than for nontraditional products.

The second additional method for avoidance or evasion is through FDI accounts. A multinational enterprise with operations in Brazil could respond to the attractiveness of Brazilian assets by holding a larger part of its liquid balances in Brazil. Conceivably, such firms could go even further and take funds from investors with the intention of investing them in Brazil, but the potential for the authorities to take harsh countervailing actions is generally sufficiently unpleasant to make such evasion unlikely on a meaningful scale. Foreign investors may also attempt to mislabel their investments as FDI when their intention is to purchase Brazilian financial assets, but such activities can be countered by requiring proof that transactions described as FDI ultimately result in the purchase of real assets.

A third method for avoidance or evasion is through the use of trade credit, which has traditionally been exempt from capital controls (although the rationale for such exemptions is less clear now that emerging markets are experiencing excessive capital inflows). A foreign bank could offer a side payment (a polite term for a bribe) to a Brazilian bank to say that some of the credits being extended to Brazilian exporters were being made by the foreign bank, allowing the foreign bank to remit the funds to Brazil and use them to purchase Brazilian assets.

The final method for avoidance or evasion is to operate through alternative exchange markets. In Brazil, in addition to the official market, there are both a legal tourist market and an illegal parallel market. Foreign tourists also have the right to buy *reais* on the official market, and since bank spreads are higher, the *real* is normally at a discount in this market. Although this provides some incentive for foreign investors to use the tourist market, doing so would be illegal (and the limited capacity of the tourist market makes it also impractical). The *real* tends to be at an even bigger discount in the illegal parallel market than in the tourist market, but it would be distinctly risky for a foreign investor to bring money in through the parallel market, not least because it would be impossible to take it out again. Therefore, there is unlikely to be significant leakage through either of these other exchange markets in Brazil. Late in 2011 exchange pressures eased and the Brazilian authorities announced the end of capital controls for the time being.

2

The Case for Prudential Capital Controls

The era of financial globalization has brought to developing and emerging-market economies a succession of booms and busts in capital flows, of which the recent crisis is only the latest episode. What distinguishes the latest crisis is that it primarily affected the financial systems of advanced economies, which has raised broader questions about the optimality of laissez-faire and the scope for domestic and international regulation in finance. From this point of view, the recent resurgence in the use of prudential controls on capital inflows by developing and emerging-market economies can be viewed as the international equivalent of the type of macroprudential policies that have been advocated since the crisis to deal with excessive swings in credit and asset prices.

An economist's reaction to every call for public intervention is to ask what market inefficiency is targeted for remedy. In the case of global capital flows, this question is addressed by the "new theory" of prudential capital controls, which we review in this chapter. The main point is that optimal prudential controls correct distortions that lead economic agents to take too much risk when there is a boom in capital inflows. However, as we point out in the last part of the chapter, the fact that controls may be corrective should not be taken as a blanket endorsement of capital controls in general. Extensive capital controls on inflows—for example, like those implemented by China—are difficult to justify on prudential grounds and seem instead aimed at maintaining a persistent undervaluation of the Chinese currency. It is important, thus, to make the distinction between *corrective controls* (which correct a distortion) and *distortive controls* (which create a distortion).

The "New Theory" of Prudential Capital Controls

The recent theoretical literature on booms and busts in capital flows provides some guidance about prudential capital controls. This literature examines whether free capital flows to developing and emerging-market economies are desirable from the perspective of improving overall welfare when there are booms and busts in capital flows (Korinek 2010, 2011; Jeanne and Korinek 2010a, 2010b). It identifies precisely the externalities involved in booms and busts and the appropriate policies to mitigate those externalities.

The ebbs and floods of capital flows to developing and emerging-market economies are determined by a number of factors, including the risk appetite of foreign investors (sometimes tainted by irrational exuberance), the returns available in mature markets, and the global business cycle. These factors contribute to create a capital flow cycle marked by booms and busts. This cycle is amplified by mechanisms that have been highlighted and analyzed in the "third-generation" approach to currency and financial crises.[1] A boom in capital inflows is associated with a buildup in external debt, a real appreciation of the domestic currency, and a general rise in the price of domestic assets. Those developments mutually reinforce each other, as the rise in the dollar value of domestic assets increases the "internationally acceptable collateral" on the basis of which domestic agents can borrow abroad. Instead of simply cooling down the economy through a trade channel, the real exchange rate appreciation magnifies the country's ability to finance its growth through external credit.

The problem is that long booms in capital flows are often followed by a sudden stop, during which the same amplification mechanisms work in reverse. The sudden capital outflow is associated with a depreciation of the currency and a decline in the price of domestic assets. The bust is amplified by a fire sale of domestic assets on the part of overleveraged domestic borrowers seeking to repay their external creditors, leading to further downward pressure on the exchange rate, financial stress, a debt crisis, and bankruptcies. The real exchange rate depreciation then causes real disruption resulting from currency mismatches on balance sheets. The vicious circle at work in the deleveraging circle is illustrated in figure 2.1 (borrowed from Korinek 2011).

The financial amplification mechanisms depicted in figure 2.1 illustrate how the fluctuations in capital flows to developing and emerging-market economies can be particularly virulent and can generate boom-bust cycles that are much more volatile than the typical business fluctuations in advanced econo-

---

1. To simplify, the first-generation approach to currency crises blamed the crisis on country macroeconomic policies that are inconsistent with the maintenance of the fixed peg (Krugman 1979). The second-generation approach emphasized the self-fulfilling nature of speculation and "market spirits" (Obstfeld 1996). The third-generation approach, spawned by the balance-of-payment crises of the 1990s in emerging-market economies, gave center stage to currency mismatches and, more generally, to balance-sheet fragilities (Aghion, Bacchetta, and Banerjee 2004).

Figure 2.1   Deleveraging externalities in an open economy

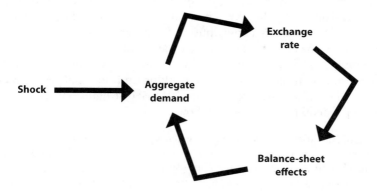

Source: Authors' illustration.

mies.[2] A negative demand shock tends to depreciate the domestic currency, which in turn has an adverse balance-sheet effect on domestic agents that are indebted in foreign currency and amplifies the decrease in demand. This amplification mechanism can involve other shocks, including for example a decrease in foreign investors' appetite for domestic assets. It also can involve other channels without currency mismatches. For example, Olivier Jeanne and Anton Korinek (2010a) outline how capital outflows reduce the price of a domestic asset that is used as collateral, so that adverse balance-sheet effects can arise even if the external debt is denominated in domestic currency. Joshua Aizenman (2011) presents a model in which the amplification comes from contagious runs in the banking system.

The feedback mechanisms shown in figure 2.1 explain not only why capital flows to developing and emerging-market economies may be very volatile, but also why they may be excessively volatile from a social welfare point of view, thus justifying corrective public intervention. This comes from a simple externality: Individual rational agents (if they are small) do not internalize their contribution to aggregate systemic risk when they design their balance sheets to achieve a certain combination of risk and return. Market participants take the probability of a systemic crisis and its magnitude as given—as indeed they should since systemic risk does not depend on the actions of a single participant. What market participants do not take into account is that their actions jointly determine the degree of financial fragility in the economy.

From this perspective, systemic fragility is "an uninternalized by-product of external financing just as air pollution is an uninternalized by-product of driving" (Korinek 2011, 526). Large capital inflows "pollute" emerging-market

---

2. However, the global financial crisis showed that the advanced economies also can be subject to extreme fluctuations.

economies with systemic risk. The appropriate policy response therefore is fundamentally the same as textbook policies to deal with pollution or global warming: The optimal policy is a Pigouvian tax that will make private market participants internalize their contributions to systemic risk in order to restore the efficiency of the decentralized market equilibrium.[3]

The rationale behind such policy interventions is essentially the same as for macroprudential regulation of the banking and financial sector. Samuel Hanson, Anil Kashyap, and Jeremy Stein (2011, 3) distinguish microprudential and macroprudential regulation as follows:

> A microprudential approach is one in which regulation is partial-equilibrium in its conception and is aimed at preventing the costly failure of individual financial institutions. By contrast, a macroprudential approach recognizes the importance of general-equilibrium effects, and seeks to safeguard the financial system as a whole.

A macroprudential approach, in other terms, aims at making agents internalize their contribution to systemic risk, especially when there is excessive leveraging and deleveraging during credit booms and busts. Macroprudential regulation is naturally countercyclical because systemic risk builds up during credit booms and unwinds during busts.[4] Similarly, the objective of prudential capital controls is to curb the destabilizing systemic impact of booms and busts in capital flows. At the conceptual level, the case for prudential capital controls is the same as for macroprudential regulation in a domestic context.

The new theory identifies the main features of an optimal system of prudential capital controls (although the details of optimal individual policies will vary with the underlying theoretical model):

- Prudential capital controls should apply to capital inflows, as opposed to outflows, since it is excessive inflows that create vulnerability. (Controls on outflows can be used to mitigate the flight of capital and the exchange rate depreciation in a crisis, but this is a response to the crisis, not a prudential measure.)

- Prudential controls, whether they are price based or not, should be differentiated according to the contribution to systemic risk of each type of capital flow. The effective tax rate should be higher on debt flows than on equity flows, higher on short-term or foreign-currency debt than on long-term or domestic-currency debt, and zero or close to zero on FDI, which has few if any adverse systemic consequences.

---

3. The appropriate intervention does not necessarily have to be implemented through a tax; it could involve quantitative restrictions or trading "permits" for issuing certain kinds of liabilities. Regardless of the form, such interventions can be considered, in reduced form, as an effective tax on capital inflows.

4. Countercyclicality in capital adequacy ratios is the feature emphasized in banking regulators' definition of "macroprudential."

Table 2.1 Externalities imposed by different financial instruments in Indonesia, 1998 (percent)

Asset category	Optimal tax rate with 100 percent probability of sudden stop in capital inflows within 12 months	Optimal tax rate with 5 percent probability of sudden stop in capital inflows within 12 months
Dollar-denominated debt	30.7	1.54
GDP-indexed dollar debt	26.8	1.34
CPI-indexed rupiah debt	14.1	0.71
Rupiah-denominated debt	8.9	0.44

CPI = consumer price inflation

Notes: Optimal tax rates are calculated to maximize overall welfare given a 100 or 5 percent probability of a sudden stop in capital inflows.

Source: Korinek (2010).

- Prudential controls also should be tuned to the variations in systemic vulnerability over time. The optimal Pigouvian tax is countercyclical: Its effective rate should increase during capital flow booms and be reduced to zero during busts or when capital flows are too small to generate systemic risk.

Calibrated versions of various models tell us something about the size of the optimal Pigouvian tax. Anton Korinek (2010) calibrates a stylized model in which sudden stops in capital flows give rise to the vicious deleveraging circle shown in figure 2.1. He calibrates the model to the experience of Indonesia before and during the Asian crisis and determines the optimal rate of taxation on various types of debt flows. The second column of table 2.1 reports the optimal Pigouvian tax on various types of debt (all with a maturity of one year) when one knows for certain that a sudden stop is going to occur during the following year. The third column reports the optimal tax rate if a sudden stop is expected to occur with a probability of 5 percent. Korinek's results illustrate that the tax rate should be higher on systemically more dangerous forms of debt (for example, dollar-denominated debt).

Javier Bianchi (2011) quantifies the optimal tax in a dynamic model of a small open economy calibrated to emerging-market economies. He assumes that all capital inflows take the form of debt with a maturity of one year and denominated in foreign currency. Unlike Korinek (2010) Bianchi does not make the optimal tax rate dependent on the type of capital inflow, but his model is more dynamic and yields results on how the optimal tax should vary over time.

Bianchi finds that the relationship between the capital flow cycle and the optimal tax is highly nonlinear (figure 2.2). The optimal tax rate on debt inflows is zero when foreign debt is lower than 26 percent of GDP because in this case the country is not vulnerable to a bust with a deleveraging externality.

Figure 2.2   Optimal tax rate on one-year foreign currency–denominated debt

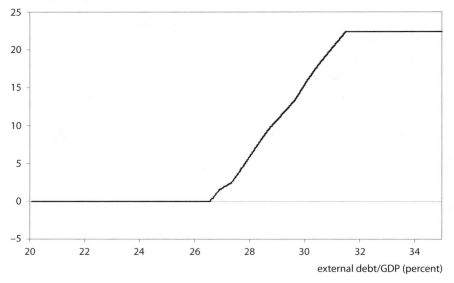

tax rate (percent)

Note: The variable on the horizontal axis is the ratio of debt to total GDP; Bianchi (2011) reports instead the ratio of foreign assets to tradable GDP, which in his calibration amounts to one-third of total GDP.

Source: Bianchi (2011, figure 3).

The optimal tax rate sharply increases if the country is in a region of vulnerability where its external debt-to-GDP ratio is between 26 and 32 percent, reaching a maximum tax rate close to 22 percent. Interestingly, the optimal tax rate stops increasing if debt exceeds 32 percent of GDP. In this case, the tax increase necessary to reduce the debt level would be so large that it is preferable to simply let the country run up against its external debt constraint. The average tax rate, taken over a large number capital flow booms and busts, is close to 4.5 percent.

Ricardo J. Caballero and Guido Lorenzoni (2009) consider whether developing and emerging-market economies should resist appreciation of their currency during a boom (modeled as a positive shock in domestic demand) in order to protect the export sector. Such policies may be justified, in their model, if the export sector is financially constrained. The rationale for public intervention is that erosion of the country's export capacity implies that there will be excessive exchange rate overshooting when the boom comes to an end. Caballero and Lorenzoni look specifically at how to mitigate this inefficiency using consumption taxes, but a tax on capital inflows would have a similar effect.

These results should be taken with a large grain of salt because the underlying assumptions of these three models are simplistic in several ways. In particular, all households in the economy are assumed to be identical—that is, there is no inequality—following the so-called representative agent assumption (which is often criticized as an unrealistic feature of modern macroeconomic models). To the extent that real world financial crises are associated with an increase in inequality and that inequality is deemed undesirable, the models likely underestimate the optimal tax rate.

Common Objections to Prudential Capital Controls

Prudential controls on capital inflows are not new, having been used in one form or another by several countries in the 1990s, most notably Chile, but they continue to elicit a number of objections:

- Capital controls are ineffective because they are routinely circumvented.
- Controls have costly unintended consequences for the countries that impose them.
- Other policy tools should be used.
- Capital controls have adverse multilateral consequences, specifically because they impede the necessary rebalancing of global demand.

We consider these objections in turn.

Objection 1: Capital controls are ineffective because they are routinely circumvented. Furthermore, circumvention is made easier by financial development. This is a theme that runs through much of the literature on capital controls. Because market participants quickly find ways of circumventing them, it becomes a race between regulation and circumvention, which regulation ultimately loses.

The question, in our view, is not whether controls are circumvented. Surely there is some evasion, as with any form of taxation or control meant to discourage a potentially profitable private activity. However, no sensible person believes that taxes generally should not be imposed because they are to some extent evaded. The relevant question is not whether controls are evaded, but whether the extent of evasion is such as to make the controls ineffective or too costly.

A related objection is that, by providing an opportunity for government officials to collect rents, capital controls breed corruption and undermine public institutions. Again, the risk of corruption does not seem to be a good enough reason to exclude capital controls a priori from the policy toolkit. Here, the relevant question is instead how the risk of corruption can be minimized through appropriate governance.

There is not a lot of empirical evidence to assess the performance of prudential capital controls when used on a sustained, consistent basis throughout

Box 2.1 Chile's experience with unremunerated reserve requirements (URRs) during the 1990s

For some years in the mid-1990s anyone bringing loan capital into Chile was obliged to deposit 30 percent of the value of the loan in the central bank for one year and did not receive any interest payment on that deposit. This URR was called *encaje* ("strongbox" in Spanish). Because this requirement was not made contingent on the duration of the investment in Chile, the effective tax rate was higher on short-term investments than on long-term investments, and therefore the URRs should have led to an increase in the maturity of the debt inflows.

Those controls were phased out in 1998, at the same time that a large litera-ture was emerging that took a skeptical to negative view of their effectiveness. Many of these studies argue that the controls did not affect the total volume of capital inflows and did not increase Chile's monetary independence (Edwards 1999; Gallego, Hernández, and Schmidt-Hebel 1999; and De Gregorio, Edwards, and Valdés 2000). However, some studies (e.g., Le Fort and Lehmann 2000) did find that the controls had a robust impact on total inflows. On the other hand, these studies generally conceded—even those by the critics—that the controls were effective in extending the maturity of Chile's foreign debt.

One problem with this literature, as argued by John Williamson (2000), is that the tests of the controls' success or failure are often misspecified. For example, some authors interpret the fact that the controls raised the level of domestic in-terest rates as a sign of failure (Gallego, Hernández, and Schmidt-Hebbel 1999), but this could as readily be a sign of the increased independence of monetary policy. Furthermore, the finding that the capital inflows did not increase in spite of higher interest rates suggests that the controls also had a moderating influ-ence on the total volume. Finally, one reason the impact of the capital controls is hard to detect empirically may simply be that their effects were small relative to the considerable amount of noise surrounding the overall level of capital flows and exchange rates.

the capital flow cycle. The most significant case, and the one that has been studied most thoroughly, is the experience of Chile with unremunerated reserve requirements (URRs) during the 1990s. The literature on these Chilean capital controls presents a wide array of opinions and conclusions, which are summarized in box 2.1. As one of us has argued elsewhere (Williamson 2000), the skepticism toward the Chilean capital controls generally has been over-done. On balance, the controls appear to have had some success, certainly in tilting the composition of inflows toward less vulnerable liability structures and perhaps in influencing the total volume of inflows.

The lessons from the Chilean experience are consistent with those from a broader sample of countries. Nicolas Magud, Carmen Reinhart, and Kenneth Rogoff (2011) review a large number of country experiences and empirical studies and conclude that capital controls on inflows seem to make monetary policy more independent, alter the composition of capital flows, and reduce real exchange rate pressures (although the evidence here is more controversial).

Jonathan D. Ostry, Atish Ghosh, Karl Habermeier, Marcos Chamon, Mahvash Qureshi, and Dennis Reinhardt (2010) summarize the findings of 19 country and cross-country studies, covering Chile and other countries including Brazil, Colombia, Malaysia, and Thailand. Colombia enforced the same type of controls as Chile but for a shorter period of time, from 1993 to 1998, whereas Brazil levied a tax on foreign loan inflows from 1993 to 1997. Malaysia and Thailand also experimented with controls on inflows in the mid-1990s, but for relatively short periods of time. The studies included in their sample addressed at least one of the following questions: (1) Did the capital controls reduce the volume of net flows? (2) Did the controls change the composition of flows? (3) Did the controls reduce real exchange rate pressure?

On the one hand, a clear majority of the studies included by Ostry et al. (2010) (about four-fifths) find that controls altered the composition of inflows, in particular by reducing the share of short-term debt. On the other hand, there is little evidence that controls on inflows had a systematic impact on the total volume of inflows or on the exchange rate. A majority of the studies that looked at total net flows—and about two-thirds of those that scrutinized the exchange rate—found that capital controls had no impact. This lack of evidence could reflect a reverse causality problem if the countries that imposed controls were those that were facing larger inflows for other reasons. It could also reflect the fact that the monetary authorities use the greater policy autonomy offered by capital controls to change other policies. For example, capital controls could be expected to show little impact on the exchange rate if the monetary authorities increased the interest rate more than they would have in the absence of controls. Neither source of bias has been convincingly eliminated in the literature.

Objection 2: Controls have costly unintended consequences for the countries that impose them. This objection is in some sense the opposite of the previous one: The problem with capital controls is not that they are ineffective but that they have a significant negative impact.

This line of argument is developed in a few recent microeconomic studies that look at the impact of lifting or imposing capital controls on the domestic financial and productive sectors at the firm level. The literature on stock market liberalization (which is reviewed in more detail in chapter 4) finds that the firms that become eligible for foreign ownership experience a significant decline in their average cost of capital (see, for example, Chari and Henry 2004). Conversely, Kristin Forbes (2005) argues, also based on microeconomic evidence, that capital controls tend to reduce the supply of capital, raise the cost of financing, and increase financial constraints for domestic firms. Francisco Gallego and Leonardo Hernández (2003) and Kristin Forbes (2007b) find evidence that the Chilean *encaje* affected smaller publicly traded firms more than the largest firms. Mihir Desai, C. Fritz Foley, and James R. Hines Jr. (2006) find that multinational affiliates located in countries with capital controls face higher interest rates on local borrowing than affiliates of the same parent borrowing locally in countries without capital controls.

From the point of view of the new theory of capital controls, however, what these findings suggest is that the controls produce precisely their intended effects. The main purpose of prudential capital controls is to restrain borrowing by domestic firms during a boom because the debt buildup is considered socially excessive. The fact that capital controls affect small and large firms differentially may simply reflect the latter's greater ability to circumvent the controls.

A related objection to capital controls is that they reduce the market discipline exerted on domestic policies by the threat of a costly capital flight—they loosen the "golden straightjacket," as Tom Friedman (2000) put it. But the cross-country evidence does not suggest that unfettered capital mobility actually exerts any considerable disciplining influence on domestic policies (Tytell and Wei 2004). Furthermore, it can be convincingly argued, on both theoretical and empirical grounds, that the credibility of domestic policies is better achieved by strengthening domestic institutions than by exposing the economy to balance-of-payments crises.

On balance, we think there is evidence suggesting that controls on inflows may achieve some prudential benefits, in part by shifting the composition of capital inflows toward less risky types of liabilities. Admittedly, the evidence is not overwhelming, one way or the other—prudential controls on inflows have not been used by a sufficiently large number of countries for a long enough time period or consistently enough to firmly establish or dispel their usefulness. From this perspective, we see no reason for the international community not to encourage (within bounds) the new wave of experimentation with prudential controls as a way of learning more about this important policy area.

Objection 3: Other policy tools should be used. Several policy instruments are cited in recent policy debates as being preferable alternatives to capital controls: domestic macroprudential regulation, reserve accumulation, and monetary (or fiscal) policy.

Why use capital controls instead of domestic macroprudential regulation? After all, according to the new theory, financial instruments should be taxed according to their contribution to systemic risk (a form of macroprudential regulation), not according to whether those instruments are held by residents or nonresidents. Similarly, if surges in capital inflows induce a currency appreciation that excessively weakens the export sector, the most natural instrument to deal with this problem is to subsidize the export sector rather than to tax capital inflows. What is the case for using capital controls as opposed to these instruments? There are several possible answers to that question.

First, the contribution of a given instrument to systemic risk may indeed depend on the residency of the holder if foreign investors have a stronger propensity than residents to take their money out of the country in a crisis.

What matters for systemic risk is not the overall maturity of debt per se, but how much short-term debt is liquidated instead of being rolled over during a crisis. To the extent that foreign investors contribute more to the risk of a debt rollover crisis, they should be taxed more than residents for holding the same short-term claims.

The empirical evidence supporting this argument, however, is mixed. Woochan Kim and Shang-Jin Wei (2002) find that foreign investors did not engage in more herding behavior than their onshore counterparts in Korea during the 1997–98 Asian crisis. Alexander D. Rothenberg and Francis Warnock (2006) find that almost half the sudden stops in net capital flows are actually episodes of "sudden flight" by local investors. This also means that about half are caused primarily by foreign investors (despite the fact that foreign investors normally hold far less than half the total assets), so prudential capital controls remain an appropriate instrument to deal with this type of event. Furthermore, the negative externalities associated with a sudden flight by domestic investors could be mitigated by imposing controls on outflows during a crisis.[5]

A second answer to the question of why capital controls should be used instead of other policy tools is that capital controls may fill some gaps in domestic macroprudential regulation (Ostry et al. 2011). The official sector and international bodies, such as the Basel Committee on Banking Supervision and the Financial Stability Board, have adopted rather restrictive views of macroprudential regulation, effectively limiting such measures to the inclusion of countercyclical elements in regulations governing the capital adequacy of banks. However, the logic behind macroprudential regulation should apply to all financial flows in the economy and not only to those intermediated by banks. That would include mortgages in the household sector and the choice between debt and equity finance in the corporate sector. In particular, corporations often borrow abroad on their own accounts without going through domestic banks. This means that the macroeconomic impact of capital controls may be more broad-based and far-reaching than that of banking regulation. From this point of view, prudential capital controls should be viewed as one of the many tools for macroprudential regulation in open economies.

There is another reason to view capital controls as part of the overall continuum of domestic macroprudential tools: Diversification may enhance compliance and effectiveness. As noted, capital controls give rise to circumvention efforts, but so do domestic financial regulations in general. Therefore, regulatory intervention should not be excessively intense at any point of the financial system. A relatively wide array of instruments should be used, all in moderation, to lean against excessive risk taking in both the financial and the real sectors. Capital controls are one of the instruments that can be used at the margin, alongside other macroprudential tools.

---

5. Controls on outflows no doubt would have to be much more constraining than the prudential controls on inflows in order to be effective.

Another popular alternative to prudential capital controls is the accumulation of international reserves. The central bank can accumulate reserves during a boom in order to mitigate both the appreciation of the domestic currency during the boom and its depreciation during the bust. However, the impact on the exchange rate of additional reserves is unlikely to be large if the change in reserves is sterilized and if there is free capital mobility. The exchange rate will be affected, according to the textbook model, through a portfolio effect, as the monetary authorities increase the supply of domestic-currency assets to private investors by the amount of the sterilized interventions. However, given the amounts involved, this is unlikely to have a large impact in financially integrated economies.[6]

The domestic authorities can also serve another objective by accumulating reserves: enhancing financial stability by enabling them to lend in last resort in foreign currency. In a capital flow reversal, the reserves can be lent (at the precrisis exchange rate) to domestic borrowers who cannot roll over their short-term foreign currency debt. However, providing such a financial safety net might end up encouraging domestic borrowers to borrow more in foreign currency—and at shorter maturities—during the boom, in order to obtain preferential access to liquidity in the bust. Thus, prudential accumulation of reserves would end up encouraging "bad" capital inflows in good times—an effect exactly opposite of the primary aim of prudential controls. Another problem with sterilized interventions is that they may entail a nonnegligible quasifiscal cost (whereas a tax on inflows raises fiscal revenues). In sum, sterilized changes in reserves are unlikely to be a good substitute for prudential controls on inflows.

Unsterilized changes in reserves—or equivalently, changes in the monetary policy interest rate—are a different matter. The dilemmas involved in appropriately setting the interest rate during a surge in capital inflows are well known. On the one hand, restraining growth in domestic demand and domestic credit requires an increase in the interest rate, which also appreciates the exchange rate. On the other hand, resisting the appreciation of the currency requires a lower interest rate, which amplifies the boom in demand and domestic credit. Thus it is impossible, using monetary policy, to simultaneously address the excessive appreciation of the currency and the excessive growth in domestic credit—the twin problems associated with a surge in capital inflows.

The relationship between monetary policy and prudential capital controls should probably be viewed in terms of complementarity rather than substitutability. One benefit of using capital controls on inflows is that they relax the external constraint on monetary policy and thus extend the domestic monetary

---

6. For example, the accumulation of reserves by the Central Bank of Brazil in 2010 ($57 billion) amounted to less than 5 percent of the Bovespa market capitalization at the beginning of 2010. Such interventions are much more effective in economies with a closed capital account because the accumulation of reserves affects domestic demand (as explained below in the discussion of Chinese capital account policies).

authorities' room to maneuver. With controls on capital inflows, an increase in the monetary policy interest rate has less impact, other things equal, on capital inflows or the exchange rate. The central bank can implement a countercyclical interest rate policy with fewer side effects in terms of exchange rate and capital flows, and thus monetary policy can be used more effectively to "lean against the wind" during booms in capital inflows.[7]

For all these reasons, we view prudential capital controls as a legitimate tool in the panoply of policies available to deal with booms and busts in capital flows. Capital controls are no panacea, but neither are the other policy instruments that are often used for similar purposes. Overall, capital controls and these other instruments should be considered more like complements than substitutes. First, capital controls can be viewed as one component of macroprudential regulation. Second, they increase the effectiveness of reserve accumulation or monetary policy in dealing with surges in capital inflows. From this point of view, there seems to be no good reason to characterize capital controls as a tool of last resort to be used only when all other options have been exhausted, as the staff of the International Monetary Fund does in its recent analytical work on this topic (IMF 2011; Ostry et al. 2010, 2011).[8]

Objection 4: Capital controls have adverse multilateral consequences, specifically because they impede the necessary rebalancing of global demand. If capital controls are effective in reducing net inflows and currency appreciation, they also reduce demand in the countries that impose them, and thereby reduce global demand. This is costly for the rest of the world, especially when there is insufficient global demand, as now in the wake of the Great Recession. Achieving full employment at the global level requires a rebalancing of demand from the low-saving, high-deficit countries toward the high-saving surplus countries, which would be enhanced by the surplus countries letting more capital flow in from the deficit countries. From this point of view, controls on capital inflows could create a new impediment to the rebalancing of global demand.

This objection has merits, but we do not think it has great force against the kind of prudential controls discussed here. A moderate tax on capital inflows of the type that Brazil has introduced cannot have a very large impact on real exchange rates and on the volume of net capital inflows. Under reasonable assumptions, the impact on the real exchange rate cannot exceed the rate

---

7. That monetary policy can be used to achieve prudential stabilization goals does not mean that it should be. There is an ongoing debate about the role of the interest rate in financial stability. The dominant opinion among central bankers seems to be that monetary policy should continue to focus on macroeconomic objectives, and that financial-stability goals should be the focus of macroprudential policy.

8. The papers coming out of the IMF do not speak with one voice on this. IMF (2011) is strongest in stating the "last resort" view, but the papers by Ostry et al. (2010, 2011) are more nuanced, recognizing that controls may be applied earlier in cases where the flows bypass the regulated financial system.

of the tax—that is, a tax on capital inflows of x percent cannot "undervalue" the real exchange rate by more than x percent (see the appendix to this chapter, which summarizes the arguments in Jeanne 2011). For example, although the Brazilian capital controls may have limited the appreciation of the Brazilian currency, the magnitude of the change (a few percentage points) should have a negligible effect on global demand.

However, this objection has clear merits concerning countries that have closed capital accounts, such as China.[9] The countries with the heaviest capital account restrictions, both before and after the global financial crisis, do not seem to use them for prudential reasons. The seven countries that had the most restricted capital accounts in 2005, according to an index developed by Martin Schindler (2009), were Angola, China, India, Russia, Sri Lanka, Tanzania, and Tunisia. The capital controls in these countries do not have the features of prudential controls described above; instead, they are comprehensive, are not price based, and are not countercyclical.

The case of China deserves special consideration because it may be the biggest contributor to future global imbalances, as shown in figure 2.3. This figure shows current account surpluses for all the countries that had surpluses in 2003–05, according to the IMF's *World Economic Outlook* (WEO) database, excluding oil-exporting countries (which are removed because they accumulate foreign assets for reasons that are specific to their country circumstances, which are well understood). The data cover 2000–15, and so the last third of the figure represents a forecast by the IMF staff.

In this group, the "sudden-stop" countries are those that either had a sudden stop in capital inflows between 1995 and 2000 or benefited from a swap with the US Federal Reserve or other central bank in 2008.[10] These are developing and emerging-market economies that are relatively open to international capital flows and thus are typical candidates for using prudential capital controls to smooth the volatility in capital flows. The figure shows the share of the surplus that comes from those countries, from China, and from the other surplus countries (which include Germany and Japan).

Figure 2.3 highlights two striking facts. First, the sudden-stop countries account for a small and decreasing share of the current account imbalances. In other words, the countries that are likely to implement prudential controls do not significantly contribute to global imbalances. The second striking fact is the size of China's contribution to global surpluses, especially looking forward. The WEO predicts that by 2015 China will account for more than 60 percent of the global surplus (excluding oil exporters). If capital account policies matter for global imbalances, China should be the focus, not the developing and emerging-market economies that are relatively open to capital flows.

---

9. For a description of the Chinese capital account regime, see Lardy and Douglass (2011) or Prasad and Wei (2007).

10. A sudden stop is defined as a decline in the financial account of more than 5 percent of GDP. The list of sudden stops comes from Jeanne and Rancière (2011).

Figure 2.3   Global current account surpluses by country source, 2000–15

billions of dollars

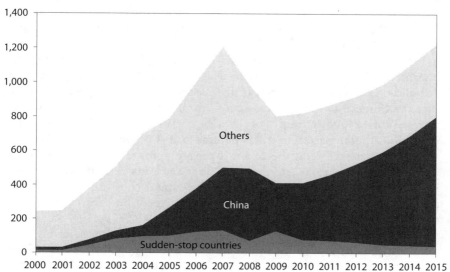

Notes: Figure shows aggregate current account surpluses for all countries that had surpluses in 2003–05. Sudden-stop countries are those that had a sudden stop in capital inflows between 1995 and 2000 or benefited from a swap with the US Federal Reserve or other central bank in 2008.

Source: International Monetary Fund, *World Economic Outlook* database, October 2010.

There is an argument that China's capital account policies, defined in a broad sense to include accumulation of foreign assets by the public sector, are essential to understanding why China has such a large current account surplus (Jeanne 2011). Think of an open economy in which the government uses two policy instruments. First, the government determines the volume of gross capital inflows using capital controls. Second, the public sector accumulates a large stock of foreign assets. It stands to reason that adjusting these two instruments enables the country to control the level of net capital flows. Essentially, the controls on capital inflows prevent the accumulation of foreign assets by the public sector from being offset by capital inflows to the private sector.

If the government controls the country's volume of net capital flows, then it also controls the current account balance. From there, it is easy to see that the government also controls the trade balance and that the real exchange rate must be at the level consistent with the trade balance. Note that the effectiveness of this policy would be considerably reduced if the government relied solely on one instrument (either foreign asset accumulation or controls on capital inflows) and that it is the combination of the two that makes it possible to control the real exchange rate.

This is not the customary way to present Chinese policies. The more conventional view is that the Chinese central bank resists the nominal appreciation of the renminbi through foreign exchange interventions. This conventional view misses one important point, however: If the Chinese authorities were only buying reserves, they could resist the nominal appreciation of the renminbi, but not the real appreciation, which would still come about through domestic inflation.

Where controls on capital inflows come into play is by preventing the internal appreciation of the renminbi. This is achieved by repressing domestic demand or, equivalently, by increasing the saving rate. Indeed, one can argue that the Chinese authorities induce a form of "forced saving" within China through their capital account policies. One way of understanding this is that the Chinese public sector, at the same time as it is purchasing large volumes of foreign assets, is forcing the domestic private sector to buy large volumes of yuan-denominated assets (sterilization bonds and bank deposits) that cannot be sold to foreign investors because of the capital controls. The domestic income that is spent on those assets cannot be spent on consumption, and therefore is a form of forced saving.

Obviously, there are other explanations for the high Chinese saving rate, ranging from the lack of social insurance to the demographic aging of the population to the underdevelopment of the financial sector.[11] Using these explanations, the required reforms should be to "increase social insurance, strengthen corporate governance, and implement reforms to increase access to credit for households and SMEs [small and medium enterprises] in China" (Blanchard and Milesi-Ferretti 2009, 17). However, to the extent that the high Chinese saving rate is due to its capital account policies, the focus instead should be on giving foreign investors greater access to Chinese financial assets, which should have a much more rapid impact on the Chinese exchange rate than the other structural reforms.

The discussion on the relationship between capital controls and real exchange rate undervaluation extends beyond China. Figure 2.4 shows a systematic relationship between the extent of controls on capital inflows, as measured by Schindler's index (2009), and currency undervaluation, as measured by Simon Johnson, Jonathan Ostry, and Arvind Subramanian (2010).[12] The figure reports, on the horizontal axis, the extent of currency overvaluation (a negative number implies that the currency is undervalued) and, on the vertical

---

11. On the lack of social insurance, see Chamon and Prasad (2010). On financial underdevelopment, see Caballero, Farhi, and Gourinchas (2008) or Song, Storesletten, and Zilibotti (2011).

12. Johnson, Ostry, and Subramanian (2010) run a cross-section regression of the log of a country's price level relative to the United States on the country's per capita GDP for every year. This regression captures (in a cross-section context) the Balassa-Samuelson effect, which predicts that as countries grow richer, the real exchange rate generally appreciates. The measure of undervaluation or overvaluation reported in figure 2.4 is the average residual from this regression, i.e., the deviation of a country's real exchange rate from the level expected after correcting for the Balassa-Samuelson effect.

Figure 2.4 Correlation between controls on capital inflows and exchange rate misalignment, emerging-market economies, 2000–05

extent of controls on capital inflows (Schindler index)

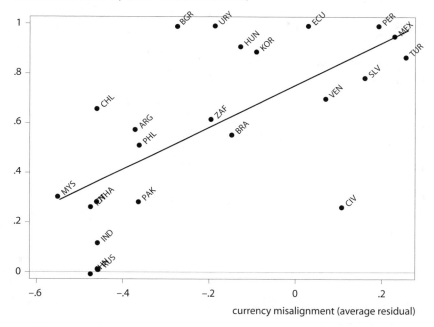

currency misalignment (average residual)

Notes: The horizontal axis shows the extent of currency overvaluation (values less than zero indicate undervaluation). The vertical axis shows the extent of capital flow liberalization (lower numbers imply more restrictions on capital inflows). See table 3A.1 for country abbreviations.

Sources: Extent of controls on capital inflows from Schindler (2009); currency misalignment (under- or overvaluation) from Johnson, Ostry, and Subramanian (2010).

axis, a measure of capital flow liberalization (a low number implies that capital inflows are heavily restricted) for emerging-market economies. The positive correlation indicates that countries with heavier restrictions on capital inflows tend to have undervalued currencies. This correlation cannot be accounted for by prudential capital controls on capital inflows since no country was implementing such controls during the period under consideration (2000–05).

Distinguishing between Corrective and Distortive Capital Controls

This analysis should make clear that the case for prudential controls should not be misconstrued as a broad endorsement of capital controls or a call for enhanced use of capital controls in general. In fact, most existing capital

Figure 2.5 Behavior of the real exchange rate with corrective versus distortive capital controls

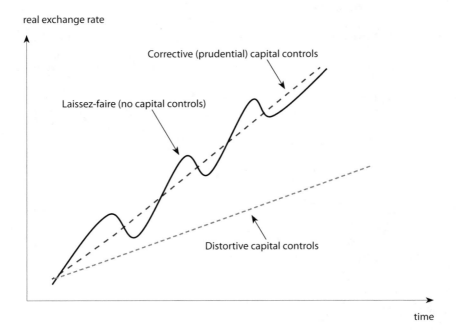

real exchange rate

Corrective (prudential) capital controls

Laissez-faire (no capital controls)

Distortive capital controls

time

Note: This figure is purely illustrative and is not based on a calibrated model.

Source: Authors' illustration.

controls are not prudential in the sense used here and may distort capital flows in harmful ways.

It is important to make the distinction between corrective and distortive capital controls. Capital controls can play a corrective role because capital flows are sometimes excessive, when they reflect irrational exuberance or induce systemic fragilities that are not internalized by market participants. But capital flows may also be a warranted response to secular changes in economic fundamentals; in these cases, there is no clear prudential reason for resisting the resulting currency appreciation.

The difference between prudential (or corrective) capital controls and distortive capital controls is illustrated by figure 2.5, which shows the behavior of the real exchange rate without controls (solid line) and with controls (dashed lines) in a hypothetical emerging-market economy. The behavior of net capital inflows (not shown) would be very similar to that of the real exchange rate.

The purpose of prudential controls, as illustrated by the figure, is to smooth fluctuations in capital flows and in the real exchange rate, which would be excessive under laissez-faire. Controls symmetrically reduce the magnitude of the fluctuations, during both the boom and the bust, but they do not distort the average level of the real exchange rate or of net capital inflows over the course of a correctly anticipated cycle.

By contrast, distortive controls introduce a persistent wedge between the equilibrium real exchange rate and the "shadow" real exchange rate, defined as the counterfactual exchange rate, which would be observed in the absence of intervention.[13] The wedge is not zero on average. In figure 2.5 the shadow rate is labeled "laissez-faire." The line labeled "distortive capital controls" illustrates the case of a country that resists the real appreciation of its currency and maintains an increasing gap between the real exchange rate and the equilibrium shadow rate. Although the observed real exchange rate appreciates over time, it does so at a lower level than the shadow rate, and the gap between the two widens over time.

Dani Rodrik (2008) argues that a persistent real exchange rate undervaluation can be justified to underpin an export-led development policy if the export sector generates positive growth-inducing externalities. Even if one accepts the empirical evidence behind this claim (a source of diverging views, including among us), attempting to exploit such positive externalities through a competitive exchange rate is problematic in several ways. First, to the extent that such externalities also exist in other countries, this is essentially a beggar-thy-neighbor approach since the country that undervalues its currency raises its growth at the expense of its trade competitors—which may be mostly other developing countries. It would be preferable to exploit the externalities using other tools that are more multilaterally beneficial, such as domestic industrial policies (Rodrik 2010). Second, this approach reduces overall global demand. These considerations may perhaps be left aside if the country undervaluing its currency is small, but they become of first importance to the international community if the country is a strategic participant in the global trade system.

In the long run, a strategy of persistent real undervaluation is self-destructive because it undermines the very free trade system required to reap the benefits from this strategy. The current status quo is characterized by an asymmetry between the strong international rules for trade in goods in place through the World Trade Organization and the quasi absence of international rules for trade in assets. This asymmetry is difficult to defend because, as shown in Jeanne (2011), a country can use capital account restrictions to manipulate its real exchange rate in a way that reproduces the effects of a combination of tariff and subsidy. Thus, the lack of international discipline over the policies that affect exchange rates—among which capital account policies figure prominently—may ultimately weaken the international support and consensus for free trade itself.

---

13. The term "shadow" real exchange rate is borrowed from the first-generation models of currency crises (Flood and Garber 1984). In those models, the shadow exchange rate is the exchange rate that would be observed if the central bank let the currency float (i.e., maintained a constant level of foreign exchange reserves). Note that unlike the fundamental equilibrium exchange rate (FEER), the shadow exchange rate is not based on a norm for the current account balance.

Appendix 2A

Effect of Capital Controls on Exchange Rates

Olivier Jeanne (2011) uses a dynamic optimization model to analyze the impact of a control on capital inflows on the exchange rate of a small open economy. The control takes the form of a Brazilian-style tax on the purchase of domestic assets by nonresidents that is proportional to the amount of the transaction and does not depend on the length of time the assets are held. The model shows that the tax can be used to undervalue the real exchange rate, but that under plausible conditions the rate of undervaluation cannot exceed the rate of taxation. This result is derived through two lines of reasoning (involving the long run and the short run, respectively). These are explained below, using the example of international investors evaluating the dollar return from investing in a small open economy whose currency is the peso.

For examining the effects in the long run, assume that the capital control is introduced today and is expected to be relaxed at some point in the future, say, in 10 years. Another assumption (which will be relaxed shortly) is that other things remain equal, specifically, that the introduction of the capital control affects neither the peso interest rate yield curve today nor the exchange rate that will prevail in 10 years, and therefore the capital control reduces the dollar return on a 10-year peso investment by the amount of the tax. For the dollar return on this investment to revert to the precontrol level, the peso must depreciate today by the same amount as the tax, in order for the return loss due to the tax to be exactly offset by the expected appreciation of the peso. Thus, other things equal, the peso has to depreciate by the amount of the tax in order for 10-year peso bonds to yield the same dollar return as before.

Of course, other things are not equal, and additional effects must be taken into account that cut different ways. On the one hand, depreciation of the peso today will lead to accumulation of net foreign assets while the controls are in place and so the peso should appreciate during the next 10 years. The capital control also tends to depress domestic demand today relative to the future, which should be associated with an increase in the 10-year real interest rate on peso bonds. Both effects will appreciate the peso today and thereby mitigate the impact of the capital control on the exchange rate. On the other hand, the expectation that the control might be reintroduced in the future may depreciate the peso. On balance, it is unclear that those second-round effects make the real exchange rate more or less responsive to the tax.

The short-run reasoning for Jeanne's conclusion that the rate of undervaluation cannot exceed the rate of taxation involves the risk of speculative inflows leading to an abrupt revaluation of the peso. A persistent undervaluation makes speculating on the appreciation of the currency a one-sided bet for long periods of time. This makes the currency vulnerable to a speculative attack that in turn would lead to capital inflows and the revaluation of the currency (the examples of this include Germany in 1973).[14] With a closed capital account, it is impossible to speculate on an appreciation of the currency, but if the capital control takes the form of a tax, speculators weigh the potential gains from participating in the attack against the cost of the tax.

To capture this channel, Jeanne (2011) assumes that the domestic authorities have an upper limit on their holdings of foreign assets (reserves). If foreign assets exceed that limit, the authorities stop accumulating them and let the exchange rate "float" to the unconstrained level that would prevail without the capital control. In this case, too, there exists a direct relationship between the size of the tax and the size of the currency undervaluation sustainable by the control. More precisely, the amount of sustainable undervaluation should be equal to the size of the tax on capital inflows.

This relationship stems from the fact that the speculation is essentially a round trip through which foreign investors buy domestic currency assets at the undervalued exchange rate in the hope of reselling them at the appreciated shadow exchange rate after a successful attack. Their potential return is the amount of the appreciation, whereas their cost is the tax that has to be paid on the purchase of the domestic currency assets. As long as the appreciation remains lower than the tax, foreign investors are dissuaded from speculating on an appreciation. But if the expected appreciation is larger than the tax, speculating is a profitable one-way bet, and it is only a matter of time before foreign investors coordinate a successful attack. The maximum size of the currency undervaluation that can be sustained by the domestic authorities is thus equal to the tax rate in this case too.

---

14. See Grilli (1986) for a first-generation model in which the speculative attack leads to a revaluation of the currency.

3

Capital Account Liberalization and Growth

If you torture the data long enough, it will confess.

—Ronald Coase (2001)

This chapter examines the correlation between a country's long-run growth and development and its integration into the global financial system. The key question addressed is whether and to what extent there is any robust correlation between capital account liberalization and medium- to long-run growth. The analysis involves a "meta-regression" approach that measures the robustness of the results across a large number of empirical specifications.[1] The analysis fails to produce robust evidence of a positive relationship between financial globalization and growth, raising questions about the pursuit of all forms of international financial integration as an urgent policy goal.

Snapshot of Long-Run Trends

Figures 3.1 through 3.4 plot the long-run relationship between the globalization of capital and financial markets (here termed "financial globalization") and economic growth and development. They plot countries' GDP per capita (in market exchange rate–valued US dollars at 2000 prices) against two widely used measures of financial globalization: a de facto or outcome-based measure of each country's international financial assets and liabilities (figures 3.1 and 3.2) and a de jure measure of each country's policy stance toward financial globalization as measured by Dennis Quinn and Maria Toyoda (2008) (figures 3.3 and 3.4).

All four figures indicate a strong positive correlation between long-run development and a country's financial globalization (the correlations between

---

1. Table 3A.1 lists the countries included in the analysis (and the country abbreviations used).

Figure 3.1 De facto financial globalization and development, all countries, 2007

log of GDP per capita

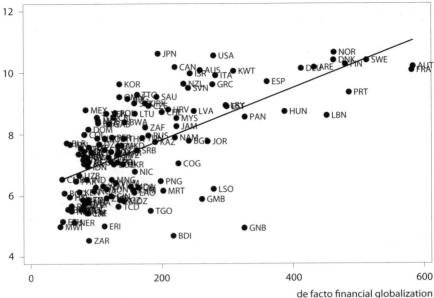

de facto financial globalization
(stock of external financial assets and liabilities as share of GDP)

Source: Authors' calculations.

income and financial globalization are 0.62, 0.7, 0.59, and 0.71, respectively).[2] The two key questions are: First, does this correlation hold for shorter time periods such as 5, 10, 20, and 40 years—that is, do capital account liberalization policies show an impact on growth during these shorter durations? The second and perhaps more important question is whether the causation runs (1) from financial globalization to long-run growth and development, (2) in the other direction, from growth to financial globalization, or (3) from other variables that affect both growth and financial globalization? Before we turn to these questions, we provide some background on the recent efforts to extend financial globalization.

---

2. The strong positive relationship continues to hold in figures 3.1 and 3.2 even when the outliers in terms of extent of financial globalization are eliminated.

Figure 3.2 De facto financial globalization and development, advanced and emerging-market economies, 2007

log of GDP per capita

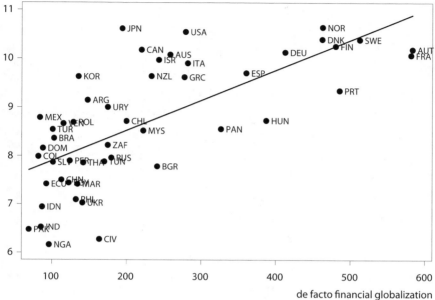

de facto financial globalization
(stock of external financial assets and liabilities as share of GDP)

Source: Authors' calculations.

Push for Capital Account Liberalization during the 1990s

A little over a decade ago, just before the Asian financial crisis of 1997–98, there was a consensus among leading macroeconomists that it was time for developing economies to liberalize their capital accounts. In a famous speech during the International Monetary Fund's Annual Meetings in 1997, the IMF's First Deputy Managing Director Stanley Fischer stated the case for financial globalization and advocated an amendment to the IMF's Articles of Agreement, the purpose of which "would be to enable the Fund to promote the orderly liberalization of capital movements."[3] Yes, there were risks associated with opening up to capital flows, but Fischer was convinced that these were more than offset by the potential benefits. Rudiger Dornbusch, having written eloquently and convincingly on the usefulness of financial transactions taxes just a short while earlier (Dornbusch 1996), now characterized capital controls as "an idea whose

---

3. Stanley Fischer, "Capital Account Liberalization and the Role of the IMF," speech at the Annual Meetings of the International Monetary Fund, September 19, 2007.

Figure 3.3 De jure financial globalization and development, all countries, 2007

log of GDP per capita

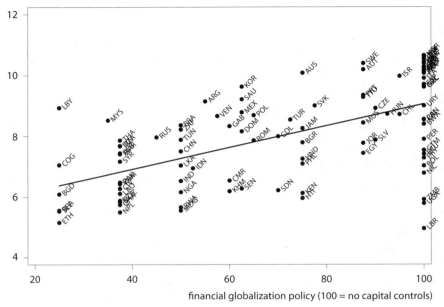

financial globalization policy (100 = no capital controls)

Source: Authors' calculations.

time is past." He wrote, "The correct answer to the question of capital mobility is that it ought to be unrestricted" (Dornbusch 1998, 20).

At the time, there was little systematic evidence that the theoretical benefits of capital flows would in fact be realized. One could look at the reduction in financing costs available through access to international markets or the competitive gains from the domestic presence of foreign banks—as Fischer did in his IMF speech—and conclude that the gains were already apparent. Or one could look at the still-fresh Mexican peso crisis of 1994–95 and the Asian financial crisis which was then under way and conclude that the potential costs were too high. Nonetheless, so strong was the theoretical consensus in favor of capital account liberalization that many presumed, as Fischer did (2003, 14), that the evidence of its benefits would accumulate over time, as the evidence of the benefits of trade liberalization had done a couple of decades earlier.[4]

---

4. The Asian financial crisis forced the IMF to abandon the effort to amend its Articles of Agreement to promote capital account liberalization. But the United States has continued to promote such measures and has succeeded in getting several of its trading partners to agree to them in recent bilateral trade agreements, including Chile and Singapore.

Figure 3.4   De jure financial globalization and development, advanced and emerging-market economies, 2007

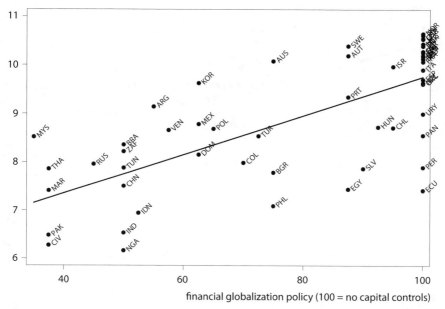

log of GDP per capita

financial globalization policy (100 = no capital controls)

Source: Authors' calculations.

After the onset of the Asian financial crisis, the IMF's approach to capital flows took a more nuanced turn: A liberal capital account was not unambiguously good at all times and in all places; countries should decide this for themselves, taking account of context and circumstance. But the tenor of the IMF's views remained in favor of capital account liberalization. The IMF never argued that countries should be cautious of foreign capital. Instead, the line was that foreign capital remained fundamentally beneficial and that reaping the benefits of financial globalization required a series of complementary reforms such as macroeconomic stability and a sound and well-regulated financial system.[5] Effective capital account liberalization was thus a question of proper sequencing.

And then in 2008 came the global financial crisis, which particularly affected, at least in the short run, a number of countries in eastern Europe that were large net importers of foreign capital. Figure 3.5 shows the correlation between growth during the crisis and net private capital flows before the crisis for a group of emerging-market economies (the nature of this relationship over longer periods is discussed in greater detail below).

---

5. This view is expressed well in Mishkin (2006).

Figure 3.5 Relationship between net private capital flows before the 2008 financial crisis and growth during the crisis for emerging-market economies

change in growth (percent)

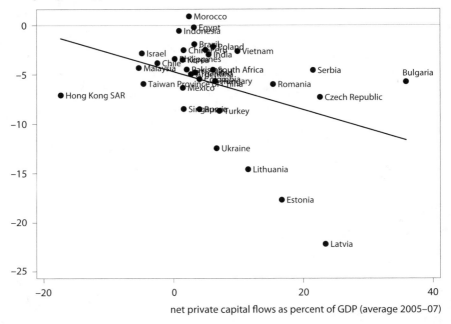

net private capital flows as percent of GDP (average 2005–07)

Note: Change in growth is calculated as average GDP growth in 2008–09 minus average GDP growth in 2005–07.

Source: Authors' calculations.

In 2009 the IMF again reassessed the issue and for the first time shed its long-standing ideological stance in favor of foreign capital: "For both macroeconomic and prudential reasons, therefore, there may be circumstances in which capital controls are a legitimate component of the policy response to surges in capital inflows" (Ostry et al. 2010, 15). The principle is elaborated:

> A key conclusion is that, if the economy is operating near potential, if the level of reserves is adequate, if the exchange rate is not undervalued, and if the flows are likely to be transitory, then use of capital controls—in addition to both prudential and macroeconomic policy—is justified as part of the policy toolkit to manage inflows. Such controls, moreover, can retain potency even if investors devise strategies to bypass them, provided such strategies are more costly than the expected return from the transaction: the cost of circumvention strategies acts as "sand in the wheels." (Ostry et al. 2010, 5)

In the policy domain, the new conventional wisdom is thus that "capital controls are a legitimate part of the toolkit to manage capital inflows in certain circumstances." But what is the conventional wisdom in the academic domain, especially on the question of foreign capital and long-run growth?

Recent Literature

Between the Asian financial crisis of the late 1990s and the beginning of the global financial crisis in 2008, three academic studies in particular sought to reassert a positive view of financial globalization.[6] Peter Henry (2007) argues that the failure of existing studies to detect a positive impact of financial globalization on growth stems from three factors. First, the studies look for permanent growth effects whereas, in the basic Solow growth model, permanent decreases in the cost of capital and hence increases in the ratio of investment to GDP have only a temporary effect on growth. Second, much of the empirical work fails to distinguish between the effects of financial globalization on developing and on developed countries. Finally, financial globalization indicators are measured with considerable error. He then suggests that studies that address these deficiencies provide a little more favorable evidence for the positive effects.[7]

Ayhan Kose, Eswar Prasad, Kenneth Rogoff, and Shang-Jin Wei (2009), who provide perhaps the most detailed and careful review of the literature, conclude that the cross-country evidence on the growth benefits of capital account openness is inconclusive and lacks robustness. They suspect that the weakness of the macro evidence in favor of financial globalization is due to the fact that researchers have been looking in the wrong places. They argue that the effects of financial globalization are apparent not so much through the cost of capital and investment, but indirectly through "collateral benefits" such as macroeconomic discipline and financial and institutional development. Moreover, they claim there are threshold effects, with financial globalization more likely to have positive effects the higher the level of financial and institutional development and the greater the macroeconomic discipline. As Kose et al. acknowledge, this argument remains largely speculative, given that the evidence is largely suggestive and preliminary.

Frederic Mishkin's *The Next Great Globalization* (2006) presents an exceptionally well written and clearly argued case in favor of the benefits of financial globalization. He views a sound financial system as the sine qua non of economic growth: Without appropriate financial intermediation, savers cannot channel their resources to investors, and capital cannot be allocated efficiently. Hence the potential gains of financial globalization are too great

---

6. Each of these three studies is reviewed by Rodrik and Subramanian (2009).

7. Although Henry's critique of the existing literature is broad in nature, his research focuses on establishing the benefits of one type of financial globalization, namely, opening up to portfolio flows into the stock market.

to pass up. Mishkin does recognize the limitations of international financial integration: It is incomplete; international financial markets work imperfectly; capital flows can create all sorts of problems when financial institutions take excessive risks; capital account liberalization can misfire when done badly; and there are no one-size-fits-all policies when it comes to prudential regulation. In fact, much of his book is about financial globalization gone wrong, including the financial crises in Mexico (1994), South Korea (1997), and Argentina (1999) and the difficulties of undertaking financial reform. Nonetheless, he concludes that the appropriate reaction to these complications is not to delay liberalization or throw sand in the wheels of international finance, but to ensure implementation of the requisite complementary reforms. Essentially, Mishkin presents a more recent version of Fischer's 1997 case to the IMF Annual Meetings, updated to account for the intervening financial crises in East Asia and elsewhere.

In contrast to these three studies, others shifted away from agnosticism about the growth effects of foreign capital and toward a slightly more negative view. Two stand out, one by Eswar Prasad, Raghuram Rajan, and Arvind Subramanian (2007) and the other by Pierre-Olivier Gourinchas and Olivier Jeanne (2007).[8] These studies throw cold water on the presumed complementarity between foreign capital and economic growth: Countries that have grown more rapidly are those that rely less and not more on foreign capital; and, in turn, foreign capital tends to go to countries that experience not high but low productivity growth.

The latest salvo in support of financial globalization comes from our Peterson Institute for International Economics colleague, William Cline, in a comprehensive and thoroughly researched book, *Financial Globalization, Economic Growth, and the Crisis of 2007–09* (2010). Instead of conducting yet another statistical study to examine the relationships between financial globalization and growth, he undertakes a statistical meta-analysis.

Essentially, he chooses nine studies and averages the results (in a statistically valid fashion) and concludes that there is an unambiguously positive causal relationship between financial globalization and growth. His quantitative estimate is that moving from being financially closed to becoming financially open yields a long-run growth (per capita) impetus of between 1.23 and 1.99 percent per year. This is astonishingly high: In a standard Solow growth model, an extra percentage point of foreign savings as a share of GDP that finances additional domestic investment increases growth by about 0.2 or at most 0.3 percent per year. Thus, moving from being closed to open is equivalent to permanently generating extra savings and investment of between 4 and 10 percentage points of GDP permanently. Alternatively, there are other collat-

---

8. See also Aizenman, Pinto, and Radziwill (2007). Several earlier studies fail to find a significant impact of capital account liberalization on growth, e.g., Rodrik (1998) and Edison et al. (2002). The literature on international financial integration and growth is too large to be reviewed here in detail; see Eichengreen, Gullapalli, and Panizza (2011) or Obstfeld (2009) for recent reviews.

eral benefits that generate total factor productivity growth of an equivalent amount.

We have reservations about the Cline meta-analysis approach. Among other deficiencies, the studies are selectively chosen; the studies included are plagued by a host of specification and statistical deficiencies (for example, none effectively addresses the endogeneity of financial globalization); and the sample is restricted to currently advanced economies and emerging-market economies.

"Meta-Regression" Approach

But instead of retreading old ground, we retain some of the flavor of the meta-analysis in Cline (2010) in trying to assess the current literature without running two million regressions à la Xavier Sala-i-Martin (1997).

We identify seven essential ways in which existing studies differ and then examine the results for all combinations of these seven sources of difference in current studies of the financial globalization–growth relationship.

1. Measuring Financial Globalization

Current studies use various proxies for financial globalization. First, there are de jure measures, which capture government policies toward financial globalization. The source for identifying policies is typically the IMF's *Annual Report on Exchange Arrangements and Exchange Restrictions* (AREAER) database. These policies are combined in different ways to create a measure or index of financial globalization. We use three widely used de jure measures from Menzie Chinn and Hiro Ito (2008), Dennis Quinn and Maria Toyoda (2008), and Abdul Abiad, Enrica Detragiache, and Thierry Tressel (2008).

Second, there are de facto measures of financial globalization based on stocks of foreign capital in different countries. The most widely used measure is from Philip Lane and Gian Maria Milesi-Ferretti (2007), who compiled a database of actual financial flows and then used these flows to derive stocks of foreign assets and liabilities in a given country. Most of the current literature measures financial globalization using the total stocks of assets plus liabilities as a share of GDP.

Third, there are de facto measures based on net flows instead of gross stocks (see Prasad et al. 2007 and Gourinchas and Jeanne 2007). The argument for using net flows, as discussed by Henry (2007), is that the basic Solow growth model provides insights about financial globalization based on net flows (foreign savings) not on gross flows. Moreover, net flows are important because one of the channels through which capital affects growth is the exchange rate. Net flows are captured from the capital account or, alternatively, the current account deficit (net of aid flows).

In sum, there are a total of six measures of financial globalization (at the aggregate level), three de jure measures and three de facto measures.

2. Levels or Changes in Financial Globalization

Having quantified financial globalization (using a de facto or de jure measure), it is necessary to consider what the underlying question is: Is long-run economic growth affected by the level of openness to financial globalization? Or is long-run economic growth affected by changes in openness? If it is the level that is important, should we specify globalization as the average level over which the analysis is conducted, or the level prevailing at the start of the period under examination? Using the former raises concern about reverse causality: Growth itself will affect financial globalization, and so specifying the average value will bias the results.

In sum, we have three ways of specifying financial globalization: as a change, as an initial level, and as an average.

3. Disaggregating Financial Globalization

The literature on financial globalization suggests that, in addition to the magnitude of flows and the policy measures affecting such overall flows, the type of foreign capital flows is also important. There are three key types of foreign capital: foreign direct investment (FDI); portfolio flows to domestic bond and equity markets; and debt. Our data allow us to distinguish the effects of capital flows in the following six categories: portfolio debt (also bond) flows, portfolio equity flows, FDI, nondebt flows (an aggregation of portfolio equity flows and FDI), net bank flows, and other investment flows (which comprise net bank flows and trade credits).[9] Each of these six categories can be expressed as a stock or a flow.

In sum, there are 12 disaggregated measures of financial globalization consisting of either a stock or a flow for these six categories.

4. Time-Horizon Estimation Methodology

Recent studies use various time horizons, including the 20-year period beginning in the mid-1980s (Edwards 2001 and Arteta, Eichengreen, and Wyplosz 2001), a 40-year period beginning with 1970 (Prasad, Rajan, and Subramanian 2007), and shorter five-year periods within this longer horizon (Quinn and Toyoda 2008). For completeness, we include four time horizons: 1970–2007, 1985–2007, 1990–2007, and five-year intervals beginning in 1970.

Methodologically, there is an important difference between the first three time horizons and the sequence of five-year intervals. The first three lend themselves to cross-sectional analysis, through which the variation between countries is used to tease out the overall effects of financial globalization on growth. The five-year intervals lend themselves to panel data analysis, through which

---

9. Not all six categories are disaggregated for all the analysis. For example, bond and equity flows are sometimes aggregated together.

the variation within countries across time is used to exemplify the specific interrelationships between financial globalization and growth.

For the cross-sectional approach, the relevant question is, Do countries with greater levels of financial globalization grow faster on average? For the panel data approach, the question is, Does a country grow faster during periods of more rapid financial globalization than during periods of less rapid financial globalization? One advantage of using panel data is that, at least in principle, the estimation procedure tries to correct for the endogeneity bias resulting from the fact that growth itself can have a positive impact on financial globalization, both by attracting foreign capital flows and by making policymakers more willing to liberalize policies toward foreign capital flows.

In sum, we have two estimation methodologies: cross-sectional and panel data analysis. The cross-sectional analysis can be conducted over three different time periods, and the panel data analysis can be conducted for five-year intervals within a 40-year time horizon.

It is worth pointing out that the early literature on finance focused on estimating cross-sectional relationships. Since the early 2000s, however, greater emphasis has been placed on panel estimation methodologies for the reasons noted above. Sala-i-Martin (1997) has tested the robustness of variables for the cross-sectional context, but there have not been any similar exercises for the panel estimation procedures. Therefore, one broader contribution of our work is to test the robustness of the relationship between financial globalization and growth in a panel estimation context, which could have wider applicability to other uses of this approach to test the impact of other variables on growth.

5. Threshold Effects

Some studies argue that the effects of financial globalization are not uniform.[10] In particular, countries that implement supporting policies and institutions to improve their governance and financial institutions are more likely to benefit from financial globalization. We attempt to capture such threshold effects by comparing the financial globalization–growth relationship for different groups of countries: advanced economies, emerging-market economies, and the full sample of countries.

In sum, we have three different samples, two based on income level and one aggregate.

6. Conditioning Variables

A problem common to all econometric analysis is the omitted variables bias. How do we know that the effect that we are trying to capture is due to the variable under study (in this case, financial globalization) and not due to some

---

10. See, for example, Alfaro, Kalemli-Ozcan, and Volosovych (2007); Arteta, Eichengreen, and Wyplosz (2001); Edwards (2001); Klein (2005); and Kose et al. (2009).

other variable that is not included in the regression? There is a bewildering array of variables that can be used to condition the regression to address this problem.

We use two specifications. For the first, which is very sparse, we use just the initial level of income and the financial globalization variable of interest as explanatory variables. This specification implicitly sheds light on whether there is a simple and unconditional correlation between financial globalization and growth.[11] In the second specification, we introduce three additional explanatory variables, which are standard conditioning variables in the literature: levels of educational attainment, trade openness, and institutional quality.

In sum, we have two ways of specifying the conditioning variables.

7. Data Sources

It has recently been pointed out that growth measurements can vary substantially across the two main data sources, the Penn World Tables and the World Bank's *World Development Indicators* (see Johnson et al. 2009). These variations can potentially impact the results of cross-country regressions.

In sum, there are two primary sources of data, and to check the robustness of our results, we use both sources in analyzing each of the other six sources of difference in the current literature that are presented above.

Conducting and Presenting the Meta-Analysis

We analyze all the combinations of the seven factors that differentiate the nine studies included in the analysis, which yields a total of 2,340 regression results. We do not report the results for all these combinations here, but instead summarize a few key statistics. First, we assess what percentage of these combinations yields results showing a positive and statistically significant relationship between financial globalization and growth. Then we probe deeper to understand which combinations are more likely to yield such a relationship. Therefore, in addition to providing results for all combinations, we also provide results for different subcombinations that shed greater light on this relationship.

The spirit of this exercise is captured in the expression, "Look Ma, no hands!" Ours is the opposite of the approach Ronald Coase (2001) refers to as torturing the data so that it makes a particular kind of confession. That is, we started with no assumptions about the financial globalization–growth relationship but with a recognition that there are different ways of analyzing it. Then, we attempted to step back and mechanically allow the data to speak. Of course, this is not a completely mechanical process because our choices

---

11. The need to include the initial level of income stems from the convergence effect, namely, that poorer countries grow faster on average than richer countries. See Barro and Sala-i-Martin (2003).

on the different combinations to study can induce some biases. However, our choices were largely dictated by the literature under study and the choices these researchers made.

In presenting and interpreting the results, we show mainly the percentage of times that results yield a significant relationship, which we define at the 10 percent confidence level. How to interpret our results is not entirely obvious. On the one hand, if the different combinations are interpreted simply as being different indications of a single underlying model, and if the results were statistically significant at the 10 percent level in only 10 percent of the regressions, then we could dismiss the significant results as spurious. That is, the share of results that are significant at the 10 percent level must be substantially larger than 10 percent to indicate that the relationship is truly significant.

On the other hand, there is no real justification for the above interpretation. The various outcomes need not all relate to one underlying model, making it less obvious how to interpret results showing the percentage of times the financial globalization variable is significant at the 10 percent level.

What is undeniable is that the greater the percentage of times that the financial globalization variable is significant (the closer this comes to 100 percent), the more confidence we can have of a causal relationship between financial globalization and growth. The lower the percentage, the more skeptical we should be.

Results: Impact of Financial Globalization on Growth

The results of the meta-regression are presented in tables 3A.2 to 3A.6. Table 3A.2 summarizes the results across all 2,340 regressions. The first line shows that the financial globalization variable is significant and correctly signed (indicating a positive correlation) about 10 percent of the time and significant and incorrectly signed (indicating a negative correlation) about 4 percent of the time. Even discounting the latter number, this is far from a ringing endorsement of the beneficial growth effects of financial globalization.

A second striking pattern is evident. Even for those cases where the financial globalization variable is significant, there are four mitigating considerations:

- The financial globalization variable is nearly twice as likely to be significant for de facto financial globalization measured in stock terms as it is for de jure financial globalization. This is consistent with endogeneity driving the positive correlation.

- The financial globalization variable is three times as likely to be significant when it is specified as a period average or period change than when it is specified as a beginning-of-period value. This is also consistent with endogeneity driving the positive correlation.

- The financial globalization variable is nearly three times as likely to be significant when other correlates are not added. This suggests that omitted variables account for a large share of the significant results.

■ The financial globalization variable is twice as likely to be significant for advanced economies than for emerging-market economies. This is consistent with a threshold effect for financial globalization, namely, that positive effects can kick in at high levels of per capita income.

A third observation is that, in contrast to the claims of Quinn and Toyoda (2008), the panel results fail to provide convincing evidence of a positive financial globalization–growth relationship. In replicating the Generalized Method of Moments (GMM) results from the Quinn and Toyoda study, we take on board the critique of David Roodman (2008), who cautions against the use of too many instruments when using GMM estimators. As he points out, with difference GMM, the problem is one of weak instruments, and with system GMM, the problem is one of invalid instruments. Roodman (2008, 27–28) recommends the following:

> To reduce the danger, several practices ought to become standard in using Difference and System GMM. Researchers should report the number of instruments generated for their regressions. In System GMM, Difference-in-Hansen tests for the full set of instruments for the levels equation, as well as the subset based on the dependent variable, should be reported. Results should be aggressively tested for sensitivity to reductions in the number of instruments. And researchers should not take much comfort in specification tests that barely "exceed conventional significance levels" of 0.05 or 0.10 as those levels are not appropriate when trying to rule out specification problems, especially if the test is undersized.

We take this on board and report the significance of results both when the Roodman (2008) specification tests are applied and when they are not. In the latter case, the financial globalization variable is significant 25 percent of the time. When other tests suggested by Roodman are also applied, the financial globalization variable is significant only 7 percent of the time, which is below the value obtained in the cross-sectional estimations.

Finally, somewhat reassuringly, portfolio equity and FDI flows are more likely to generate positive and significant impacts on growth compared with banking or portfolio debt flows. This is consistent with the results in the literature. For example, Ayhan Kose, Eswar Prasad, and Marco Terrones (2009) find evidence that FDI and portfolio equity liabilities boost productivity growth, whereas external debt is actually negatively correlated with productivity growth.

The weak effects of the impact of financial globalization and growth are illustrated in figures 3.6 through 3.9. Figures 3.6 and 3.7 plot the relationship between average growth in per capita GDP (1970–2007) and the change in the de facto measure of globalization for all countries and for a sample of advanced and emerging-market economies, respectively. In figures 3.6 and 3.7, the change in financial globalization is for the de facto, Lane and Milesi-Ferretti (2007) measure and change is measured between 1970 and 2007. Figures 3.8 and 3.9 plot the same relationship with the Quinn and Toyoda (2008) de jure measure replacing the de facto financial globalization measure. Both figures show that there is no correlation between the two variables (the correlations are, respectively, 0.17, 0.04, 0.18, and 0.05). This is the broad pattern exhibited across the range of specifications reported in table 3A.2.

Do these results indicate anything more than just that, on average, there is little evidence in favor of a strong financial globalization–growth relationship? For example, are there some particular circumstances (some combinations of the variables) that provide evidence of a stronger relationship and therefore could shed light on the overall impact of financial globalization? To this end, we decompose the results to show different combinations of the variables. The results are presented in tables 3A.3 and 3A.4 for the cross-sectional regressions and in tables 3A.5 and 3A.6 for the GMM regressions. In each case, the reported number is the percent of times that the financial globalization variable is significant at the 10 percent level for that particular combination of the financial globalization variable and the other choice variable.

Only two circumstances appear to indicate significant positive effects of financial globalization (defined arbitrarily to be when the financial globalization variable is significant at least 50 percent of the time). The first is in the advanced-economy sample, when the financial globalization variable is the aggregate de facto stock variable (total assets and total liabilities divided by GDP). This combination appears in table 3A.3. The second is when the financial globalization variable is defined as the stock of portfolio equity assets and liabilities divided by GDP and when this variable is defined in change terms or as the average value during the period under consideration (table 3A.4). The results are also generally positive when portfolio equity is defined in net flow terms. Surprisingly, the results are stronger for portfolio equity flows than for FDI flows, although we suspect that in practice the two may not be easy to distinguish.

Are there similar strong results in the panel estimations?[12] Table 3A.5 suggests that there are really no combinations that indicate a strong financial globalization–growth relationship defined as meeting the criteria suggested by Roodman (2008). But the detailed panel results for the disaggregated measures of financial globalization (table 3A.6) do indicate a strong positive relationship between financial globalization and growth for portfolio equity, especially when it is measured in flow terms.[13] It is reassuring that both the cross-section

---

12. We emphasize that we report significance only when the additional criteria proposed by Roodman (2008) are satisfied.

13. When we do not impose the two additional criteria of Roodman (2008), we obtain some combinations for which a stronger financial globalization–growth relationship is possible. This is especially true for the de jure variable, and especially when the specifications do not include the full set of conditioning variables. The interesting thing is that the strongest relationship is for the sample of all countries compared with the sample of advanced or emerging markets, implying that the relationship is strong for other developing countries. So the panel and cross-sectional results are not consistent in two ways. First, in the cross-section, it is the de facto measures that are more likely to be significant, whereas it is the other way around in the panel estimations. Second, there is evidence of threshold effects, except that in the cross-section rich countries are more likely to exhibit a positive relationship, whereas in the panel one needs the nonemerging developing countries to exhibit such a relationship.

Figure 3.6   Relationship between growth and change in de facto financial globalization, all countries, 1970–2007

average growth in per capita GDP (percent)

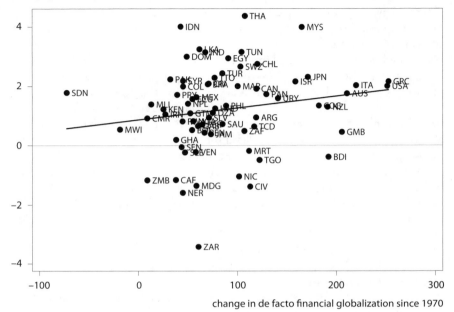

change in de facto financial globalization since 1970

Source: Authors' calculations.

and panel estimation frameworks yield consistent results for portfolio equity flows.

There is a final question to be addressed. As figures 3.1 and 3.2 show, there is a strong positive correlation between the level of income and the level of financial globalization. But our meta-analysis finds little evidence for a strong correlation between changes in the level of income (that is, growth) and changes in the level of financial globalization. How can these two findings be reconciled?

It is instructive to look at a similar pattern in another context: the relationship between democracy and development. Daron Acemoglu, Simon Johnson, James Robinson, and Pierre Yared (2008) show a similar strong correlation between democracy and development over the long run but find no relationship between changes in income and changes in democratization over time spans of 50, 100, and 200 years. They posit that this results from omission of a common factor that relates to the historical experience of colonization that occurred circa 1500, which pushed some countries along a path of high growth and democratization and others along a path of low growth and slower political development. The effect of incorporating this factor is to recover the

Figure 3.7   Relationship between growth and change in de facto financial globalization, advanced and emerging-market economies, 1970–2007

average growth in per capita GDP (percent)

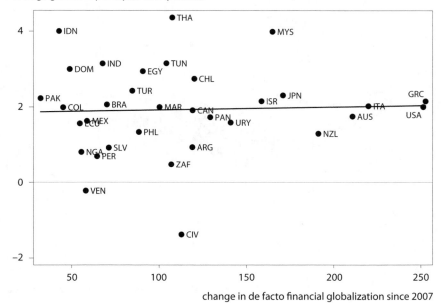

change in de facto financial globalization since 2007

Source: Authors' calculations.

correlation between changes in income and changes in democratization over a much longer time span (about 500 years).

Similarly, there could be a common factor that explains why our findings seem to suggest that there has been no impact on growth from the changes in financial globalization during the 40 years or so covered by our analysis. This factor could either reflect the impact of rising incomes on policy decisions to open the economy to capital flows, a common factor that promotes both growth and financial globalization, or a causal relationship between financial globalization to income levels. More research is necessary to extend the time horizon of this type of analysis in order to ascertain the nature and direction of relationship between financial globalization and growth and development.

In sum, our meta-analysis finds little robust evidence of a positive relationship between financial globalization and growth, except possibly for equity market liberalization. There is a lack of positive results across all the specifications: when financial globalization is measured at an aggregated or disaggregated level or measured in de facto or de jure terms; over all time periods; with all estimation methods; for all country samples; and for all the

Figure 3.8   Relationship between growth and change in de jure financial globalization, all countries, 1970–2007

average growth in per capita GDP (percent)

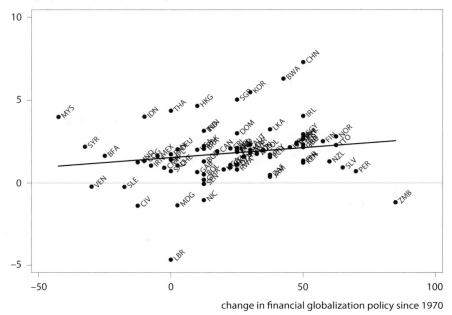

change in financial globalization policy since 1970

Source: Authors' calculations.

conditioning variables and other controls. However, even with such a uniform lack of robustness, it is true that the absence of evidence is not evidence of an absent relationship between financial globalization and growth.

Finally, it is worth examining the argument advanced by Kose et al. (2009) that there are significant collateral benefits that make financial globalization worthwhile in the absence of direct benefits for growth, including for example pressure to improve domestic macroeconomic and financial discipline and institutions. The problem is that there are few arguments to support this. For example, access to international finance often enables profligate governments to operate on soft budget constraints for longer than they could in the absence of foreign capital. Indeed, some people interpret the experience of the United States during the global financial crisis as a case of easy money and lax regulatory standards that resulted from an excess availability of foreign capital. Another example is Turkey during the 1990s. Having opened up to financial globalization in the late 1980s, the Turkish government found a ready source of cheap finance (external borrowing intermediated through domestic commercial banks) through which it could sustain a growing fiscal imbalance. In the absence of such capital, Turkey would have been forced to put its fiscal house

Figure 3.9   Relationship between growth and change in de jure financial globalization, advanced and emerging-market economies, 1970–2007

average growth in per capita GDP (percent)

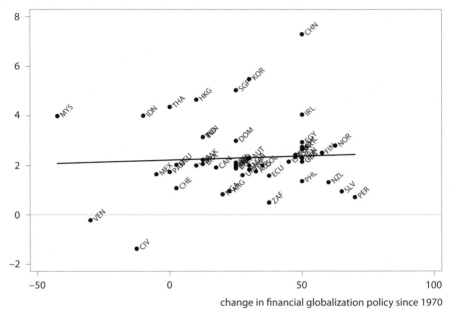

change in financial globalization policy since 1970

Source: Authors' calculations.

in order a lot sooner than in 2001, and in a much less costly manner. In fact, financial globalization can be argued to actually impede the development of domestic financial markets because domestic investors can simply shift their wealth abroad instead of pushing for institutional reform.

Even if the collateral benefits argument proves valid, the policy implications are far from clear. The best way to achieve a particular policy objective—whether it is macroeconomic stability or institutional development—is to pursue it directly, not as an indirect or incidental result of reforms in other areas. In order to make the argument in favor of financial globalization on account of its collateral benefits, it is necessary not only to demonstrate the existence of those collateral benefits, but also to demonstrate that financial globalization is a particularly effective way—among all possible reform strategies—to attain those benefits. In turn, that requires both that financial globalization have sufficiently strong first-order effects on the policy channels in question and that its administrative and other costs be less than the costs of other feasible reforms. That case has yet to be made.

Appendix 3A Tables

Table 3A.1 List of countries included in meta-analysis

Advanced countries (24)		Emerging-market economies (32)	
Country	Abbreviation	Country	Abbreviation
Australia	AUS	Argentina	ARG
Austria	AUT	Brazil	BRA
Belgium	BEL	Bulgaria	BGR
Canada	CAN	Chile	CHL
Denmark	DNK	China	CHN
Finland	FIN	Colombia	COL
France	FRA	Côte d'Ivoire	CIV
Germany	DEU	Dominican Republic	DOM
Greece	GRC	Ecuador	ECU
Hong Kong	HKG	Egypt	EGY
Ireland	IRL	El Salvador	SLV
Israel	ISR	Hungary	HUN
Italy	ITA	India	IND
Japan	JPN	Indonesia	IDN
Netherlands	NLD	Korea	KOR
New Zealand	NZL	Malaysia	MYS
Norway	NOR	Mexico	MEX
Portugal	PRT	Morocco	MAR
Singapore	SGP	Nigeria	NGA
Spain	ESP	Pakistan	PAK
Sweden	SWE	Panama	PAN
Switzerland	CHE	Peru	PER
United Kingdom	GBR	Philippines	PHL
United States	USA	Poland	POL
		Russia	RUS
		South Africa	ZAF
		Thailand	THA
		Tunisia	TUN
		Turkey	TUR
		Ukraine	UKR
		Uruguay	URY
		Venezuela	VEN

(continued on next page)

Table 3A.1   List of countries included in meta-analysis *(continued)*

	Others (92)		
Country	**Abbreviation**	**Country**	**Abbreviation**
Afghanistan	AFG	Honduras	HND
Albania	ALB	Iran, Islamic Republic of	IRN
Algeria	DZA	Iraq	IRQ
Angola	AGO	Jamaica	JAM
Armenia	ARM	Jordan	JOR
Azerbaijan	AZE	Kazakhstan	KAZ
Bangladesh	BGD	Kenya	KEN
Belarus	BLR	Kiribati	KIR
Benin	BEN	Kuwait	KWT
Bolivia	BOL	Kyrgyz Republic	KGZ
Bosnia and Herzegovina	BIH	Laos	LAO
Botswana	BWA	Latvia	LVA
Burkina Faso	BFA	Lebanon	LBN
Burundi	BDI	Lesotho	LSO
Cambodia	KHM	Liberia	LBR
Cameroon	CMR	Libya	LBY
Central African Republic	CAF	Lithuania	LTU
Chad	TCD	Macedonia FYR	MKD
Congo, Democratic Republic of	ZAR	Madagascar	MDG
Congo, Republic of	COG	Malawi	MWI
Costa Rica	CRI	Mali	MLI
Croatia	HRV	Mauritania	MRT
Czech Republic	CZE	Mauritius	MUS
Eritrea	ERI	Moldova	MDA
Estonia	EST	Mongolia	MNG
Ethiopia	ETH	Mozambique	MOZ
Gabon	GAB	Myanmar	MMR
Gambia	GMB	Namibia	NAM
Georgia	GEO	Nepal	NPL
Ghana	GHA	Nicaragua	NIC
Guatemala	GTM	Niger	NER
Guinea	GIN	Oman	OMN
Guinea-Bissau	GNB	Papua New Guinea	PNG
Haiti	HTI	Paraguay	PRY

(continued on next page)

Table 3A.1   List of countries included in meta-analysis *(continued)*

Others (92)			
Country	**Abbreviation**	**Country**	**Abbreviation**
Romania	ROM	Tajikistan	TJK
Rwanda	RWA	Tanzania	TZA
Saudi Arabia	SAU	Togo	TGO
Senegal	SEN	Trinidad and Tobago	TTO
Serbia	SRB	Turkmenistan	TKM
Sierra Leone	SLE	Uganda	UGA
Slovakia	SVK	United Arab Emirates	UAE
Slovenia	SVN	Uzbekistan	UZB
Sri Lanka	LKA	Vietnam	VNM
Sudan	SDN	Yemen	YEM
Swaziland	SWZ	Zambia	ZMB
Syria	SYR	Zimbabwe	ZWE

Note: Table includes 148 countries and excludes countries with population less than 1 million.

Sources: International Monetary Fund, *World Economic Outlook*; World Bank, *World Development Indicators*.

Table 3A.2 Summary of results on financial globalization

	Percent positive and significant (10 percent)	Percent negative and significant (10 percent)	Number of regressions
Total[a]	10 (16)	4 (5)	2,340
Time-horizon estimation methodology			
Cross-sectional regression	11	6	108 x 15 = 1,620
1970–2007	12	4	36 x 15 = 540
1985–2007	11	6	36 x 15 = 540
1990–2007	11	6	36 x 15 = 540
Panel regression (financial globalization variable is significant and regressions meet Roodman [2008] criteria for GMM estimation methodology)[b]	7 (25)	2 (4)	48 x 15 = 720
Specification of financial globalization variable			
De jure[c]	13	4	156 x 3 = 468
De facto total[d]	17	5	156 x 12 = 1,872
De facto net flows	15	5	156 x 7 = 1,092
De facto stock	20	5	156 x 5 = 780
Timing of financial globalization variable			
As initial period value	5	6	36 x 15 = 540
As average value	16	2	36 x 15 = 540
As change	13	9	36 x 15 = 540
Disaggregation of financial globalization variable			
Portfolio debt	9	5	156 x 2 = 312

Other investment	10	7	156 x 2 = 312
Banks[e]	17	1	156 x 1 = 156
Nondebt	28	5	156 x 4 = 624
Foreign direct investment (FDI)	21	5	156 x 2 = 312
Portfolio equity	35	4	156 x 2 = 312
Conditioning variables			
Convergence term and financial globalization variable	23	5	78 x 15 = 1,170
Convergence term; financial globalization variable; and education, openness, and institutional quality[f]	9	5	78 x 15 = 1,170
Sample[g]			
All countries	16	7	52 x 15 = 780
Advanced countries	22	4	52 x 15 = 780
Emerging-market economies	11	4	52 x 15 = 780
Data source			
Penn World Tables	16	5	78 x 15 = 1,170
World Bank, World Development Indicators	16	5	78 x 15 = 1,170

GMM = Generalized Method of Moments

a. The numbers in parentheses are averages across the cross-sectional and panel regressions, without imposing the condition that the panel regressions meet the Roodman (2008) criteria.

b. The numbers in parentheses relate to the regressions without imposing the condition that they meet the Roodman (2008) criteria.

c. The de jure variables are from Quinn and Toyoda (2008); Abiad, Detragiache, and Tressel (2008); and Chinn and Ito (2008), respectively.

d. The de facto variables for stocks are total foreign assets plus total foreign liabilities as a share of GDP and similar variables for debt, equity portfolio, FDI, and other investments. The de facto flow variables are total inflows and outflows (taken as a net flow) as a share of GDP and similar variables for debt, portfolio, FDI flows, and other invesments. In addition, there is a de facto variable for the net current account flows (plus aid). In all, there are 15 financial globalization variables, of which 3 are de jure, 5 are de facto stock, and 7 are de facto flow variables.

e. The subcomponent of other investment, of which the domestic counterparty is a bank.

f. Education is the average years of schooling (Barro and Lee 2010) and institutional quality is from International Country Risk Guide (ICRG) Risk Ratings.

g. The sample has 148 countries, of which 24 are advanced and 32 are emerging-market economies.

Source: Authors' calculations.

Table 3A.3 Growth and aggregated measures of financial globalization, detailed cross-sectional results (percent)

| | De facto measure | | | | | |
| | Total foreign assets plus liabilities as share of GDP | | Net total flows as share of GDP | | CAB plus ODA as share of GDP | |
Regression	sig	sig+corr	sig	sig+corr	sig	sig+corr
All regressions	22	19	13	6	13	6
Samples						
All countries	11	3	11	0	11	3
Advanced economies	56	56	19	11	11	3
Emerging-market economies	0	0	8	8	17	11
Time periods						
1970–2007	11	11	19	6	8	6
1985–2007	25	22	6	3	25	6
1990–2007	31	25	14	11	6	6
Data sources						
Penn World Tables	19	19	9	6	13	6
World Bank, World Development Indicators	26	20	17	7	13	6
Timing of financial globalization variable						
Average value	19	17	17	14	19	11
Initial value variable	17	11	3	3	11	6
Change variable	31	31	19	3	8	0
Controls						
Financial globalization + initial income	35	30	11	4	20	9
Financial globalization + initial income + education, openness, and institutions	9	9	15	9	6	2

De jure measure (index of capital account liberalization)

Regression	Quinn and Toyoda (2008)		Abiad, Detragiache, and Tressel (2008)		Chinn and Ito (2008)	
	sig	sig+corr	sig	sig+corr	sig	sig+corr
All regressions	6	4	19	10	11	6
Samples						
All countries	0	0	3	0	19	8
Advanced economies	17	11	28	17	11	8
Emerging-market economies	0	0	25	14	3	0
Time periods						
1970–2007	8	6	33	22	19	14
1985–2007	6	3	14	6	3	0
1990–2007	3	3	8	3	11	3
Data sources						
Penn World Tables	9	6	19	9	13	7
World Bank, World Development Indicators	2	2	19	11	9	4
Timing of financial globalization variable						
Average value	8	8	11	11	6	6
Initial value variable	3	3	22	19	14	3
Change variable	6	0	22	0	14	8
Controls						
Financial globalization + initial income	11	7	20	15	15	11
Financial globalization + initial income + education, openness, and institutions	0	0	17	6	7	0

CAB = current account balance; ODA = official development assistance

Note: Numbers represent the percent of time that the financial globalization variable is significant ("sig") or significant and correctly signed ("sig+corr") for a particular combination of regressions.

Source: Authors' calculations.

Table 3A.4 Growth and disaggregated measures of financial globalization, detailed cross-sectional results (percent)

	De facto measures: Subcomponents			
	Total FDI assets plus liabilities as share of GDP		Net FDI flows as share of GDP	
Regression	sig	sig+corr	sig	sig+corr
All regressions	21	14	20	12
Samples				
All countries	22	3	33	11
Advanced countries	42	39	6	3
Emerging-market economies	0	0	22	22
Time periods				
1970–2007	11	6	25	17
1985–2007	25	17	19	8
1990–2007	28	19	17	11
Data sources				
Penn World Tables	17	13	30	19
World Bank, World Development Indicators	26	15	11	6
Timing of financial globalization variable				
Average value	19	17	22	22
Initial value variable	31	11	11	11
Change variable	14	14	28	3
Controls				
Financial globalization + initial income	30	26	26	17
Financial globalization + initial income + education, openness, and institutions	13	2	15	7

	Total equity assets plus liabilities as share of GDP		Net equity flows as share of GDP	
Regression	sig	sig+corr	sig	sig+corr
All regressions	44	40	24	17
Samples				
All countries	61	61	14	6
Advanced countries	47	47	44	44
Emerging-market economies	22	11	14	0
Time periods				
1970–2007	42	42	19	14
1985–2007	47	42	28	19
1990–2007	42	36	25	17
Data sources				
Penn World Tables	41	41	24	17
World Bank, World Development Indicators	46	39	24	17

(continued on next page)

Table 3A.4   Growth and disaggregated measures of financial globalization, detailed cross-sectional results (percent) *(continued)*

	De facto measures: Subcomponents			
	Total equity assets plus liabilities as share of GDP		Net equity flows as share of GDP	
Regression	sig	sig+corr	sig	sig+corr
Timing of financial globalization variable				
Average value	58	56	28	28
Initial value variable	3	0	3	0
Change variable	69	64	42	22
Controls				
Financial globalization + initial income	52	52	33	22
Financial globalization + initial income + education, openness, and institutions	35	28	15	11

	Total debt assets plus liabilities as share of GDP		Net debt flows as share of GDP	
Regression	sig	sig+corr	sig	sig+corr
All regressions	14	11	13	3
Samples				
All countries	11	11	17	3
Advanced countries	22	19	17	0
Emerging-market economies	8	3	6	6
Time periods				
1970–2007	28	19	8	3
1985–2007	8	8	22	6
1990–2007	6	6	8	0
Data sources				
Penn World Tables	13	9	9	4
World Bank, World Development Indicators	15	13	17	2
Timing of financial globalization variable				
Average value	28	22	6	3
Initial value variable	0	0	11	6
Change variable	14	11	22	0
Controls				
Financial globalization + initial income	20	19	19	6
Financial globalization + initial income + education, openness, and institutions	7	4	7	0

(continued on next page)

Table 3A.4 Growth and disaggregated measures of financial globalization, detailed cross-sectional results (percent) *(continued)*

	De facto measures: Subcomponents			
	Total OI assets plus liabilities as share of GDP		Net OI flows as share of GDP	
Regression	sig	sig+corr	sig	sig+corr
All regressions	10	5	17	11
Samples				
All countries	6	0	8	6
Advanced countries	25	14	17	14
Emerging-market economies	0	0	25	14
Time periods				
1970–2007	17	6	6	6
1985–2007	6	6	17	14
1990–2007	8	3	28	14
Data sources				
Penn World Tables	11	4	15	7
World Bank, World Development Indicators	9	6	19	15
Timing of financial globalization variable				
Average value	14	14	14	14
Initial value variable	11	0	19	3
Change variable	6	0	17	17
Controls				
Financial globalization + initial income	19	9	15	7
Financial globalization + initial income + education, openness, and institutions	2	0	19	15

	Net banking flows as share of GDP	
Regression	sig	sig+corr
All regressions	11	9
Samples		
All countries	8	3
Advanced countries	19	19
Emerging-market economies	6	6
Time periods		
1970–2007	8	8
1985–2007	11	11
1990–2007	14	8
Data sources		
Penn World Tables	6	4
World Bank, World Development Indicators	17	15

(continued on next page)

Table 3A.4   Growth and disaggregated measures of financial globalization, detailed cross-sectional results (percent) *(continued)*

	De facto measures: Subcomponents	
	Net banking flows as share of GDP	
Regression	sig	sig+corr
Timing of financial globalization variable		
Average value	6	6
Initial value variable	6	0
Change variable	22	22
Controls		
Financial globalization + initial income	9	7
Financial globalization + initial income + education, openness, and institutions	13	11

FDI = foreign direct investment; OI = other investment

Note: Numbers represent the percent of time that the financial globalization variable is significant ("sig") or significant and correctly signed ("sig+corr") for a particular combination of regressions.

Source: Authors' calculations.

Table 3A.5 Growth and aggregated measures of financial globalization, detailed panel results (percent)

Regression	De facto measure			De jure measure (index of capital account liberalization)		
	Total foreign assets plus liabilities as share of GDP	Net total flows as share of GDP	CAB plus ODA as share of GDP	Quinn and Toyoda (2008)	Abiad, Detragiache, and Tressel (2008)	Chinn and Ito (2008)
All regressions						
Financial globalization variable is correctly signed + significant	19	21	4	15	38	15
Financial globalization variable is correctly signed + significant and meets first criterion[a]	8	13	2	4	10	6
Financial globalization variable is correctly signed + significant and meets criteria one and two[a]	8	17	0	8	13	8
Samples						
All countries	0	13	0	0	13	0
Advanced countries	25	0	0	25	0	25
Emerging-market economies	0	38	0	0	25	0
Controls						
Financial globalization variable + initial income and education	17	25	0	17	17	17
Financial globalization variable + initial income and education	0	8	0	0	8	0

Data source					
Penn World Tables	8	25	0	8	17	8
World Bank, World Development Indicators	8	8	0	8	8	8
Type of estimation					
System GMM	8	17	0	8	13	8

GMM = Generalized Method of Moments; CAB = current account balance; ODA = official development assistance

a. The first criterion includes the Arellano-Bond test for autocorrelation and the Hansen test for joint validity of all instruments. The second criterion is the Hansen test for validity of instruments of lagged dependent variable, which applies only to system GMM.

Note: Numbers represent the percent of time that the financial globalization variable is significant, correctly signed, and meets criteria one and two for a particular combination of regressions (unless stated otherwise). The controls are the same.

Table 3A.6 Growth and disaggregated measures of financial globalization, detailed panel results (percent)

Regression	Total FDI assets plus liabilities as share of GDP	Net FDI flows as share of GDP	Total equity assets plus liabilities as share of GDP	Net equity flows as share of GDP	Total debt assets plus liabilities as share of GDP	Net debt flows as share of GDP	Total OI assets plus liabilities as share of GDP	Net OI flows as share of GDP	Net banking flows as share of GDP
				De facto measures: Subcomponents					
All regressions									
Financial globalization variable is correctly signed + significant	48	29	48	50	6	21	2	29	35
Financial globalization variable is correctly signed + significant and meets first criterion[a]	4	8	23	42	6	21	0	19	29
Financial globalization variable is correctly signed + significant and meets criteria one and two[a]	4	13	29	54	8	8	0	13	21
Samples									
All countries	13	0	0	0	0	0	0	0	25
Advanced countries	0	0	63	75	25	25	0	0	0
Emerging-market economies	0	38	25	88	0	0	0	38	38
Controls									
Financial globalization variable + initial income and education	0	17	33	67	17	8	0	25	25
Financial globalization variable + initial income and education	8	8	25	42	0	8	0	0	17

Data source

Penn World Tables	8	25	42	58	8	8	0	17	25
World Bank, World Development Indicators	0	0	17	50	8	8	0	8	17
Type of estimation									
System GMM	4	13	29	54	8	8	0	13	21

GMM = Generalized Method of Moments; OI = other investment

a. The first criterion includes the Arellano-Bond test for autocorrelation and the Hansen test for joint validity of all instruments. The second criterion is the Hansen test for validity of instruments of lagged dependent variable, which applies only to system GMM.

Note: Numbers represent the percent of time that the financial globalization variable is significant, correctly signed, and meets criteria one and two for a particular combination of regressions (unless stated otherwise). The controls are the same.

4

Specific Component Flows

The regressions presented in the previous chapter confirm the findings in most of the literature that capital account liberalization does not have a very robust impact on growth, and also that certain types of capital flows are better for growth than others. This chapter reviews the empirical literature that focuses on the developmental impact of specific types of capital flow. We use the conventional classifications of foreign direct investment (FDI), portfolio equity flows, and net bank flows (but do not examine the three minor flows included in the regression analysis, which are sometimes lumped together).

Foreign Direct Investment

Conventional wisdom is that FDI benefits the recipient economy through a number of channels. First, an increase in FDI raises the domestic stock of capital, the marginal productivity of labor, and the level of real wages in the recipient economy. This effect is stronger if foreign firms are more productive than domestic ones, which is generally true in developing and emerging-market economies. The empirical literature on FDI and wage spillovers indeed finds that wages are higher in foreign-owned plants (Lipsey 2004). There is also evidence that wages tend to increase in domestic plants that become foreign owned, suggesting that the higher wage level is not merely due to foreign firms picking the best local workers (see Lipsey and Sjöholm 2002, on the case of Indonesia).

The second channel for benefits from FDI is the spillover from higher productivity of advanced-economy firms to domestic firms through a transfer of knowledge or technology. This channel is conceptually different from the wage spillover discussed above because it affects the total factor productivity of domestic firms (the efficiency with which they use all the factors of production) rather than the demand for domestic labor. It also has different policy implications. Specifically, to the extent that foreign firms do not internalize the spillovers from their entry into the market, FDI generates a positive externality, and the overall benefits to the economy may make it worthwhile for the domestic authorities to use subsidies to incentivize foreign firms to invest. The domestic authorities also may seek to magnify these spillovers by insisting that foreign firms share technology and knowledge with their domestic counterparts, perhaps in return for any subsidies received.

The literature distinguishes "horizontal spillovers," which benefit domestic competitors in the same industry, from "vertical spillovers," in which any benefits flow from multinationals to local suppliers. In both cases, the spillovers occur through a knowledge transfer, as local producers learn the technologies and management practices of multinational companies by observation or by hiring their workers. Multinational firms have an incentive to minimize horizontal spillovers that strengthen their domestic competitors, but they benefit from vertical spillovers that raise the quality of their inputs.

The view that FDI has positive spillovers is based in large part on event studies and narrative evidence. An example of horizontal spillovers is the emergence of the textile export industry in Bangladesh in the early 1980s (Rhee and Belot 1990). The large Korean conglomerate Daewoo established a textile plant in Bangladesh in 1979 and trained many of its Bangladeshi workers in Korea. Many of these workers eventually left Daewoo to set up their own garment export plants. An example of vertical spillovers is the joint venture between Suzuki from Japan and the government of India in 1981 to manufacture affordable small cars (Parikh 1997). All the car parts initially were imported from Japan, but the joint venture sparked the development of domestic suppliers and within 10 years these suppliers provided 90 percent of the parts. Theodore Moran (2002) provides many other examples of technology transfers induced by FDI.

The empirical literature, however, has generally failed to find a robust and systematic impact of FDI on domestic productivity. Moran, Edward Graham, and Magnus Blomström (2005) exhaustively review the two main lines of this literature, relying on disaggregated sectoral productivity data and macroeconomic evidence of the link between FDI and growth. The book begins with their observation that "determining exactly how FDI affects development has proven to be remarkably elusive" (p. 1).

Using plant-level data on Venezuelan firms, Brian Aitken and Ann Harrison (1999) find little evidence of horizontal productivity spillovers: The productivity of a given plant increases with the share of foreign ownership (especially for small plants), but the productivity of a domestically owned plant decreases with the share of foreign ownership in the industry. This suggests that foreigners own more productive plants but decrease the productivity of their domestic competitors, perhaps because the domestic competitors must pay the same fixed costs with a reduced turnover, or because foreign firms hire the best workers. Beata Javorcik and Mariana Spatareanu (2008) find similar results for Eastern Europe.

Table 4.1   Cross-country regression of growth on FDI inflows, 1980–2005 (percent)

Explanatory variable	Base Regression	Controlling for GDP per capita
FDI/GDP (average in 1980–2005, percent)	0.189*** (0.054)	0.186*** (0.055)
Initial GDP per capita (1980, log)		0.058 (0.134)
Constant	0.922*** (0.196)	0.448 (1.152)
Number of observations	118	118
R^2	0.008	0.008

Note: Simple ordinary least squares regression; dependent variable: average growth in GDP per capita. Heteroskedasticity-robust standard errors are in parentheses; *** indicates that the explanatory variable is significant at the 1 percent level.

Sources: Data on GDP per capita are from Penn World Table 6.3. Ratio of FDI inflows to GDP are from International Monetary Fund, International Financial Statistics database, July 2011.

On the other hand, several studies find evidence of vertical productivity spillovers flowing from foreign firms to their local suppliers. For example, Garrick Blalock and Paul Gertler (2008) report that the productivity of Indonesian firms in a given industry is positively affected by the share of the industry's output that is sold to foreign firms but not by the share of the industry's output that is produced by foreign firms. Beata Javorcik (2004) uses firm-level data from Lithuania and also finds productivity spillovers from FDI between foreign affiliates and their local suppliers. The fact that spillovers are vertical rather than horizontal is consistent with the multinational corporations' incentive to transfer technology to their local suppliers rather than to their local competitors. But it also weakens somewhat the case for subsidizing inward FDI since foreign companies are likely to internalize the gains from vertical spillovers to a larger extent than for horizontal spillovers.

FDI may contribute to economic growth, although the conditions under which this is the case are not very well identified. The countries that grow at higher rates also tend to receive more FDI inflows. A simple cross-country regression over the period 1980–2005 suggests that increasing the share of FDI inflows in GDP by 1 percent is associated with an increase in economic growth of nearly one-fifth of a percentage point (table 4.1). This correlation could reflect a positive impact of inward FDI on domestic growth,[1] but the causality

1. A positive impact of FDI on growth, even if it existed, would not be proof that FDI has productivity spillovers. It is sufficient that foreign firms have a higher productivity level for their entry to raise average productivity and thereby growth, at least transitorily.

obviously could run the other way, because high-growth countries can be expected to attract more FDI from the rest of the world. The main problem in the empirical literature, therefore, has been to tease out the causality from the correlation between FDI and growth.

Eduardo Borensztein, Jose De Gregorio, and Jong-Wha Lee (1998) make an influential contribution to this literature. In a panel study of 69 developing and emerging-market economies over the two decades from 1970 to 1989, they find that the impact of inward FDI on growth does not persist after controlling for the country's level of human capital (as measured by its average educational attainment). However, they also find that the interaction between FDI and human capital has a robust and positive impact on growth, suggesting that inward FDI stimulates growth if the recipient country has a sufficient level of education. One-quarter to one-half of the countries in their sample (depending on the specification of the regression) were above the educational threshold at which inward FDI has a positive impact on growth.

The subsequent literature confirms the fact that the impact of FDI on growth is not robust to the inclusion of the conditioning variables routinely used in modern growth regressions. Researchers deal with this fact by continuing to explore the existence of thresholds in recipient countries' "absorptive capacity" above which FDI can be expected to be associated with higher growth. For example, Laura Alfaro, Areendam Chanda, Sebnem Kalemli-Ozcan, and Selin Sayek (2004) define the threshold in terms of domestic financial development rather than educational attainment. They find that the identification of the threshold is rather sensitive to the measure of financial development and the estimation method. More distressingly, most of the countries in their sample of 71 (which included 20 advanced economies) were below the threshold and so were actually hurt by inward FDI.[2] They do not run a race to see whether the threshold is better defined in terms of financial development (their candidate) or schooling (as in Borensztein, De Gregorio, and Lee 1998). Indeed, such a race would be difficult to run because of a basic colinearity problem: The threshold variables tend to be highly correlated with each other and with any measure of economic development. This is a serious issue in drawing policy implications from the threshold approach to capital account liberalization.

The most skeptical contribution to that literature is probably the study by Maria Carkovic and Ross Levine (2005). They apply to FDI the Generalized Method of Moments (GMM) estimator that was used by Levine (1997) to successfully identify the impact of domestic financial development on growth. Based on a sample of 72 countries over the period 1960–95, Carkovic and Levine (2005) find that the exogenous component of FDI does not exert a robust, independent influence on growth, especially when trade openness is introduced as a control. This is true even when FDI is interacted with variables

---

2. The instrumental variable results presented in the second part of their study show a larger share of countries that benefit from FDI.

such as financial development or schooling, putting in doubt the existence of threshold effects. The authors suggest that previous results were biased by econometric methodologies that did not control for reverse causality as adequately as GMM.

The recent literature also emphasizes an important nuance between FDI flowing into the financial sector and nonfinancial FDI. Linda Goldberg (2007) argues that the lessons from research on manufacturing FDI apply to financial sector FDI too. She finds that financial FDI generally has had positive effects on recipient emerging-market economies, in particular by strengthening domestic regulation and supervision. This benign view of financial FDI was called into question by the recent crisis, in particular the experience of emerging Europe. Jonathan D. Ostry, Atish Ghosh, Karl Habermeier, Marcos Chamon, Mahvash Qureshi, and Dennis Reinhardt (2010) argue that some transactions recorded as financial sector FDI may instead be a buildup in intra-enterprise debt in financial firms and are thus more akin to debt in terms of riskiness.

In conclusion, anecdotal evidence suggests that FDI has had positive spillovers on domestic firms in some countries but that this effect is hard to identify in a robust way across countries and sectors. A number of researchers find a positive impact of FDI inflows on economic growth if threshold conditions are in place, but it is unclear whether these studies have adequately controlled for reverse causality, and the empirical identification of the threshold conditions remains elusive.

FDI is considered to be beneficial by the international community despite the lack of strong evidence that positive spillovers exist. As a consequence, many countries make efforts to attract FDI through the use of tax exemptions or special economic zones. This causes some concern about whether the international competition to attract FDI has resulted in incentives that are sometimes excessive.

That being said, a few countries also might benefit from relaxing capital account restrictions on FDI inflows. Overall, there do not seem to be good reasons for developing and emerging-market economies to discourage FDI inflows. FDI is more stable than other types of capital flows and thus seems to pose little risk in terms of financial stability. Furthermore, inward FDI tends to be associated with higher growth and may even have a causal impact on growth. Certain types of FDI (especially in extractive industries) may aggravate domestic political economy distortions and corruption, but the appropriate remedy is to reduce those distortions rather than to restrict FDI inflows.

In fact, a number of countries that maintain controls on inward FDI might benefit the most from reducing those controls, as shown in table 4.2, which draws on the data in the United Nations Conference on Trade and Development's *World Investment Reports*. UNCTAD ranks countries in terms of their inward FDI performance, measured by the ratio of a country's share in global FDI inflows to its share of world GDP. It also ranks countries according to their potential for attracting FDI, using variables that are expected to affect

Table 4.2 Top ten FDI underperformers

Country	FDI underperformance index, 2005–07	FDI liabilities/GDP, 2004 (percent)	Restrictions on FDI, 2006
South Korea	105	9.4	Yes
Kuwait	105	0.6	Yes
Iran	73	2.9	Yes
Russia	65	19.7	Yes
Belarus	64	9.1	Yes
Slovenia	63	28.1	No
Libya	46	6.0	Yes
Algeria	31	9.4	Yes
India	27	6.7	Yes
Philippines	24	19.0	No

FDI = foreign direct investment

Sources: UNCTAD *World Investment Report*; Lane and Milesi-Ferretti (2007); International Monetary Fund, *Annual Report on Exchange Arrangements and Exchange Restrictions.*

foreign firms' willingness to invest in the country.[3] Interestingly, for our purpose, the UNCTAD measure of the potential for attracting FDI does not include capital controls, so that gaps between performance and potential can plausibly be attributed to the presence of such controls.

We computed, for each of the 138 countries for which we had the relevant data, an "FDI underperformance index" to represent the difference between the country's ranking in terms of performance and its ranking in terms of potential. For example, South Korea has an index of 105 because it is ranked 124th by UNCTAD in terms of inward FDI performance but 19th in terms of FDI potential. The table reports the 10 countries that have the highest underperformance index.[4] The table also reports, for each country, its ratio of FDI liabilities to GDP in 2004, and whether it had controls on inward direct investment or on the liquidation of direct investment according to the International Monetary Fund's *Annual Report on Exchange Arrangements and Exchange Restrictions* (AREAER).

This approach seems to do a reasonably good job of identifying the countries that might have the most to gain from further liberalizing FDI inflows. First, all but two of the countries had restrictions on inward FDI. The two that

---

3. UNCTAD takes the unweighted average of the normalized values of the rate of growth of GDP, per capita GDP, share of exports in GDP, telephone lines per 1,000 inhabitants, commercial energy use per capita, share of research and development (R&D) expenditures in gross national income, share of tertiary students in the population, and a measure of country risk.

4. We excluded countries with ratios of FDI liabilities to total external liabilities and to GDP that were above average. This amounts to supplementing the UNCTAD's flow-based criterion with a stock-based criterion.

did not (Slovenia and the Philippines) in fact seem to have been less constrained than the rest, given that they also had relatively high levels of FDI liabilities. The eight countries that did have controls had FDI liabilities amounting to only 8 percent of GDP on average, much lower than the full-sample average of 58 percent.

Portfolio Equity Investment

The second component of capital flows we examine is portfolio equity flows, which represent the purchase by an investor of an equity holding in some foreign enterprise. The equity investor is typically a financial intermediary such as a mutual fund but can also include individuals, endowments, sovereign wealth funds, or even enterprises that intend to hold a small share of a company rather than to exercise control.[5]

Magnitude of Portfolio Equity Flows

As late as the mid-1980s there was virtually no foreign investment in the local equity markets of developing or emerging-market economies, outside of Malaysia and South Africa. Of course, there had been cross-holdings of equity investments among developed economies since before the First World War, but for some reason these never attracted the same degree of scholarly interest as equity investments in developing or emerging-market economies. The emergence of equity investments outside the developed economies that constitute the Organization for Economic Cooperation and Development (OECD) was very much a product of deliberate policies to liberalize the entry of foreign investors that were put in place by a number of emerging-market economies in the late 1980s and early 1990s.

IMF statistics for flows of portfolio equity capital to emerging-market economies from 1980 to 2010 are shown in table 4.3. The table shows an unbalanced panel of countries, namely, all the countries in each region that reported in a particular year; a balanced panel would be restricted to those countries that reported through the entire time period covered. The table shows that the first significant flow of this type of capital occurred after 1990, with only minor flows before then. The flow remained modest compared with other types of capital flows, but built up substantially after 2005. Particular regions (especially the Middle East and North Africa [MENA]) experienced outflows from time to time, but this first became a general phenomenon in 2008.

As the data show, portfolio equity flows to two major groups of emerging-market economies, Latin America and the Caribbean (LAC) and East Asia,

---

5. The traditional and internationally sanctioned dividing line between FDI and foreign equity investment is 10 percent: When a purchase takes a firm's holding above that proportion of the invested firm's shares, the investment is classified as FDI; when it is below 10 percent, it is considered a foreign equity investment.

Table 4.3   Flow of portfolio equity to emerging-market economies, by region, 1980–2010
(millions of US dollars)

Region	1980–84	1985–89	1990–94	1995–99	2000–04
Latin America and the Caribbean	–23	147	11,285	2,611	–3,120
East Asia and the Pacific	27	501	1,385	2,185	8,658
South Asia	5	11	1,807	2,068	4,703
Middle East and North Africa	–109	–624	62	90	–241
Sub-Saharan Africa	2	–269	–130	2,816	–428
Europe and Central Asia	n.a.	–24	351	1,666	1,184
Total	–98	–258	14,760	11,436	10,756

Region	2005	2006	2007	2008	2009	2010
Latin America and the Caribbean	6,319	5,732	17,047	–14,079	20,598	35,619
East Asia and the Pacific	25,655	52,593	14,122	–10,621	–9,633	27,570
South Asia	12,694	10,773	34,539	–15,363	20,711	39,190
Middle East and North Africa	2,277	–217	–4,385	–11,817	–3,753	1,163
Sub-Saharan Africa	3,398	10,816	3,130	–18,014	7,193	4,182
Europe and Central Asia	5,864	4,556	14,650	–12,686	5,264	2,818
Total	56,208	84,252	79,104	–82,581	40,380	110,543

n.a. = not available

Notes: This is an unbalanced panel, including all countries that report in a given year. Data for 2005–10 are annual numbers while the rest are averages for the five-year periods. For the full list of countries in the sample, see table 1.1.

Source: International Monetary Fund, International Financial Statistics, July 2011.

emerged during 1985–89 and became significant in 1990–94. After then, these regions followed divergent paths. LAC stumbled economically and capital flows turned negative, recovering only in 2007, while flows to East Asia grew exponentially. In fact, the Asian financial crisis drove capital flows negative for only a few months in 1997 before their growth resumed.

As inflows to LAC were reviving in 2007, they were tailing off in East Asia, even before the global financial crisis struck in 2008. South Asia became a major destination for portfolio equity capital during the 2000s. Inflows to MENA were irregular but never built up to a substantial figure. Sub-Saharan Africa was emerging as an important destination for equity capital prior to the crisis. Europe and Central Asia (ECA) experienced a large inflow in 2007, which promptly flowed out again the following year.

The marked outflows during the crisis in 2008 were not predicted by the theory that outflows will prove self-limiting as fleeing investors push down the price of equity. This suggests that domestic investors are more loyal than foreign investors and that they may buy stocks from foreigners for only a small price reduction, which supplies the foreign investors with domestic cash, which in turn could put downward pressure on the exchange rate.

Table 4.4 shows dividend payments to foreign investors by region. Unfortunately, country data on these flows are very limited but increase over time, so that the growth of dividend payments over time is in part a result of statistical quirks rather than economic realities. Nevertheless, the growth of dividend payments from derisory levels in the 1980s to quite significant levels by the late 2000s is reflective of reality, though net resource transfers were still strongly positive in 2007.[6] This of course will not be true in the long run: It is the nature of investment that the cost of servicing the capital eventually exceeds the value of new capital inflows. (Indeed, this is the basis for the theory of the debt cycle.)

Benefits and Costs of Portfolio Equity Flows

There are relatively few studies of the costs and benefits of liberalizing equity inflows. Among these, the work of Peter Henry, one of the first to extensively analyze the consequences of such liberalization, stands out. In a summary of his work (Henry 2003), he includes three diagrams, displayed here as figures 4.1, 4.2, and 4.3. These figures represent the average performance of the 18 countries that liberalized equity inflows in the late 1980s or 1990s and provide empirical evidence in favor of the view that such liberalization reduces the cost of capital, increases investment, and accelerates growth.[7] Henry also shows

---

6. Apparent from subtracting the total dividend outflows in table 4.4 from the total portfolio inflows in table 4.3.

7. Henry actually speaks of liberalizing "the capital account" instead of liberalizing "inflows of portfolio equity," but year 0 is characterized in each case by the liberalization of inflows into the stock market, not by complete liberalization of the capital account. Hence the alternative titles for the three figures are more accurate.

Table 4.4 Outflow of dividend income from emerging-market economies, by region, 1980–2010
(millions of US dollars)

Region	1980–84	1985–89	1990–94	1995–99	2000–04
Latin America and the Caribbean	–5	–4	–426	–2,789	–2,017
East Asia and the Pacific	n.a.	–143	–446	–773	–249
South Asia	n.a.	n.a.	n.a.	–78	–228
Middle East and North Africa	–12	–20	–31	–92	–105
Sub-Saharan Africa	–617	–482	–336	–497	–1,024
Europe and Central Asia	n.a.	n.a.	–31	–96	–1,121
Total	–634	–649	–1,270	–4,325	–4,744

Region	2005	2006	2007	2008	2009	2010
Latin America and the Caribbean	–3,879	–5,400	–6,227	–9,166	–7,995	–7,173
East Asia and the Pacific	–2,055	–2,269	–3,978	–8,052	–9,128	–8,049
South Asia	–138	–156	–271	–232	–145	–211
Middle East and North Africa	–180	–125	–106	–160	–180	–102
Sub-Saharan Africa	–1,860	–2,063	–3,029	–1,598	–1,185	–1,520
Europe and Central Asia	–2,083	–2,956	–4,387	–5,761	–3,243	–5,356
Total	–10,195	–12,968	–17,999	–24,969	–21,876	–22,410

n.a. = not available

Notes: This is an unbalanced panel, including all countries that report in a given year. Data for 2005–10 are annual numbers while the rest are averages for the five-year periods. Net dividends paid abroad, BOPS code 3340. The countries included in this table are as follows: Latin America and the Caribbean (12) = Argentina, Brazil, Chile, Costa Rica, Dominican Republic, Ecuador, El Salvador, Mexico, Panama, Paraguay, Uruguay, and Venezuela; East Asia and the Pacific (4) = China, Indonesia, Malaysia, and the Philippines; South Asia (2) = Bangladesh and Pakistan; Middle East and North Africa (4): Egypt, Morocco, Tunisia, and Yemen; Sub-Saharan Africa (9) = Burkina Faso, Côte d'Ivoire, Kenya, Mauritius, South Africa, Swaziland, Tanzania, Togo, and Uganda; and Europe and Central Asia (8) = Bulgaria, Georgia, Kazakhstan, Latvia, Moldova, Romania, Russia, and Turkey.

Source: International Monetary Fund, Balance of Payments Statistics (BOPS) database, July 2011.

Figure 4.1   The cost of capital falls when countries liberalize inflows of portfolio equity

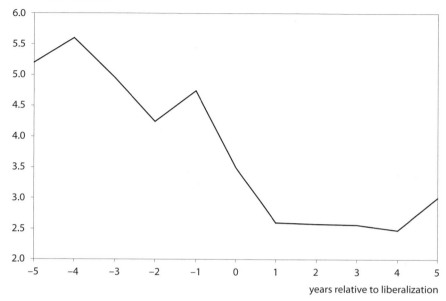

dividend yield (percent)

years relative to liberalization

Note: The 18 countries covered in this figure are Argentina, Brazil, Chile, Colombia, India, Indonesia, Jordan, Korea, Malaysia, Mexico, Nigeria, Pakistan, the Philippines, Taiwan, Thailand, Turkey, Venezuela, and Zimbabwe.

Source: Henry (2003). Reprinted with permission.

that the reduction in the cost of capital is a necessary theoretical consequence of his model, on the assumption that outflows of portfolio equity are liberalized simultaneously with inflows, but he subsequently notes that the empirical phenomenon also could have resulted from the simultaneous occurrence of other reforms.

Likewise with the increase in investment: Although such a result is expected, it is necessary to turn to other work to show that the empirical effect of liberalization on investment is positive, even after allowing for other reforms. Matters are perhaps most difficult with respect to growth, for the empirical effect (growth acceleration of 2.3 percent) is far too large to be accounted for by the induced increase in investment alone and must therefore have been reinforced by the effects of other reforms. Obviously, these empirical results are consistent with the hypothesis that equity market liberalization has a negative effect on the cost of capital and positive effects on the level of investment and the rate of growth, but they do not prove it or establish its magnitude.

Henry had in fact previously attempted to allow for the simultaneous occurrence of other reforms (Henry 2000b) in an event study that examines

Figure 4.2 Investment booms when countries liberalize inflows of portfolio equity

growth rate of the capital stock (percent)

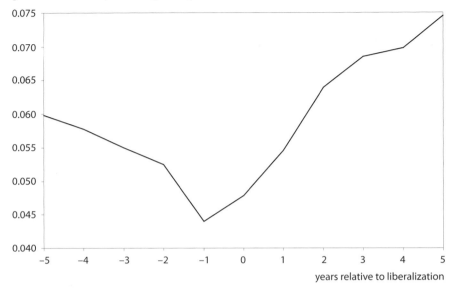

years relative to liberalization

Note: See note to figure 4.1 for country coverage.

Source: Henry (2003). Reprinted with permission.

the impact of the liberalization of entry to the stock market during an eight-month interval around the liberalization (mainly, leading up to liberalization). In his sample of 12 emerging-market economies, he shows that stock markets experienced an average abnormal dollar return of 4.7 percent per month. After allowing for the impact of comovements of world stock markets, economic policy (specifically stabilization programs, trade liberalization, privatization, and relaxation of exchange controls), and macroeconomic fundamentals, the average excess return fell to "only" 3.3 percent per month. This was still statistically significant.

In another paper, Henry (2000a) seeks to establish the link between liberalization of equity inflows and subsequent increases in investment. The problem he addresses is the empirical finding of several other economists that liberalization of the capital account did not cause a permanent increase in investment even in countries assumed to be short of capital. Henry demonstrates that theory indicates a temporary rather than a permanent increase in real investment and that the expectation of a temporary increase following the liberalization of inflows of portfolio equity is emphatically satisfied. There is, however, an alternative explanation for the finding that liberalization of inflows of port-

Figure 4.3   Growth rate of output per worker increases when countries liberalize inflows of portfolio equity

growth rate of output per worker (percent)

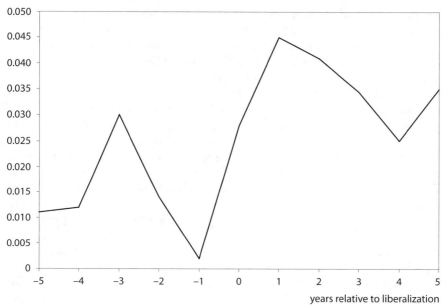

years relative to liberalization

Note: See note to figure 4.1 for country coverage.

Source: Henry (2003). Reprinted with permission.

folio investment increases real investment while liberalization of the capital account does not, and this explanation focuses on the distinction between portfolio equity and debt rather than between a temporary versus a permanent increase in investment. Under this alternative explanation, freedom of debt flows is bad for real investment, presumably because of the risk of panic-driven outflows of debt, which tends to spawn crises.

The results of Henry's studies have been further reinforced by the analysis of Geert Bekaert and Campbell Harvey (2000) and Bekaert, Harvey, and Christian Lundblad (2005 and 2006).[8] They also examine the effects of permitting foreign investors to enter equity markets. (Their proxies for the entry of foreign investors to the stock market were establishment of a country fund, the launching of American depositary receipts (ADRs), or an increase in capital flows from US investors.) They conclude that such entry reduces the cost of capital and therefore has a positive effect on the ratio of investment to GDP and hence on the growth potential of the country (Bekaert and Harvey 2000).

---

8. See also Mitton (2006).

This growth benefit is larger the greater is economic openness (that is, the ratio of trade to GDP).

Bekaert, Harvey, and Lundblad (2006) refine the analysis of these topics. Their evidence shows that liberalizing entry to the stock market accelerates the growth rate over the subsequent five-year period by slightly more than 1 percent per year. This evidence is robust to the substitution of the alternative definition of equity market liberalization that was used in Bekaert and Harvey (2000). They also find a positive coefficient on Quinn and Toyoda's (2008) measure of capital account liberalization, but not on that of the IMF (2011), which is consistent with the view that any form of equity market liberalization is advantageous to growth whereas allowing the free flow of debt is not.[9] They test whether this could be due to accompanying business-cycle effects but decisively dismiss this possibility. They devise a measure of growth opportunities that performs surprisingly well in helping to explain growth, but they show that its introduction scarcely diminished the significance of equity market liberalization. They also study the impact of both other reforms and financial development and conclude that these increased growth while diminishing but not eliminating the impact of equity market liberalization. They conclude (consistent with other evidence) that this impact is greater when countries are more financially developed (measured either by size of the banking sector or by equity market turnover) and when they have better institutions.

The evidence is therefore quite strong that it is beneficial to allow foreign inflows of equity capital, even in forms other than FDI. A critical question is whether equity market liberalization comes with costs, and if so whether those costs may be as large as (or even larger than) the benefits. The main cost is generally considered to be the risk that capital will be withdrawn in a crisis. A traditional answer has been that any attempted withdrawal is likely to provoke a decline in the stock market, which will be self-limiting, rather than to provoke a run on the currency, which tends to be self-aggravating. This raises two questions. First, is the stock market a good place for the risk inherent to life to be reflected, or is stability of the stock market an important objective? Second, may there be domestic investors who would be happy to buy stocks from foreigners for a small reduction in price, thereby giving the foreign investors currency with which to finance a run on the currency?

The first question of whether stability of the stock market is important does not appear to be addressed in the literature. It may be conjectured that the stock market is a good place for risks to be borne because, while there are quite strong links between the stock market and the real economy, these tend to operate over the long run. Household consumption is a function of the value of stock market wealth, but the short-run impact of even a large change in the stock market is fairly small. Similarly, while investment depends on the

---

9. This assumes that countries generally liberalize FDI and the flow of portfolio equity before debt flows, so that the former are caught by Quinn and Toyoda's (2008) measure, while the IMF measure basically shows the effect of freeing debt flows.

price of equity, the short-run relationship is not strong. As a result, feedback from stock prices to real activity is modest in the short run, whereas differing views about the future clearly have a major impact on investors' willingness to hold stocks. This also appears consistent with the finding of Korinek (2010) that the negative systemic externalities are smaller for equity flows than for debt flows.

The best source of information on the second question is whether crisis-induced portfolio equity outflows have caused sales of foreign exchange or a collapse of the stock market. The evidence from the Asian financial crisis and from the impact of the global financial crisis on India is that there is a mix of both effects. In both these cases, the stock markets suffered severely, but there were also currency outflows, which could occur only if domestic investors were less skittish than foreign investors and therefore sold the foreign investors the domestic currency needed to purchase foreign exchange. This is certainly the impression to be drawn from the substantial outflows of portfolio equity in 2008. On the other hand, inflows of portfolio equity investment rebounded strongly in 2009, which suggests that crisis-induced outflows are short-lived (which was also true after the Asian financial crisis).

Flow of Capital from Banks

When developing and emerging-market economies first became major borrowers on international capital markets in the early 1970s, their borrowing overwhelmingly took the form of loans from banks. Indeed, during the second half of the 1970s, it was common to refer approvingly to the process of recycling the oil surplus to developing economies.

Oil-exporting economies deposited their surpluses in banks, and the banks made medium-term loans to developing economies, which enabled them to finance current account deficits that offset the current account surpluses of the oil exporters. By and large, industrialized countries ran deficits with the oil exporters but surpluses with developing economies, enabling them to pass along the oil deficits that were anticipated in the immediate aftermath of the oil price increases of 1973.

When the debt crisis broke in 1982, it became clear that bank lending is a highly unstable source of capital and that relying on banks as intermediaries in recycling global surpluses and deficits is risky. This quickly became conventional wisdom, although the statistics in table 4.5 suggest that other components of capital flows (except perhaps FDI) are also highly volatile, notably capital outflows included in "other flows."

It is very important to distinguish sharply between two quite distinct types of bank flows: loans extended by international banks to developing economies and capital flows to developing economies from international banks that occur because they acquire banks in those countries. The latter is classified as FDI; it is more properly categorized as bank investment in developing economies, but it is not broken out separately in balance of payments statistics. Table 4.5

Table 4.5   Net flows to emerging-market economies, by region, 1970–2010 (millions of US dollars)

Region	1970–74	1975–79	1980–84	1985–89	1990–94	1995–99	2000–04	2005–09	2010
Latin America and the Caribbean	358	14,703	14,692	-15,157	37,378	65,384	21,933	59,815	132,999
FDI	-52	2,504	5,881	5,380	13,249	54,133	54,935	67,003	56,524
Equity		-3	-23	147	11,285	2,611	-3,120	7,123	35,619
Banks	68	2,170	5,598	-3,796	737	-1,417	-2,822	-4,504	35,470
Other	343	10,032	3,235	-16,888	12,107	10,057	-27,061	-9,807	5,386
East Asia and the Pacific	205	2,473	11,142	13,996	38,309	31,223	40,393	91,184	273,664
FDI	571	610	2,171	4,276	22,124	51,986	51,072	123,200	136,485
Equity	n.a.	2	27	501	1,385	2,185	8,658	14,423	27,570
Banks	27	616	372	537	4,662	-5,809	-4,881	-11,415	88,200
Other	56	1,244	8,571	8,683	10,138	-17,139	-14,455	-35,024	21,409
South Asia	n.a.	1,533	3,066	7,694	10,053	10,202	12,108	54,094	69,056
FDI	n.a.	29	110	179	807	3,460	4,478	17,784	14,633
Equity	n.a.	n.a.	5	11	1,807	2,068	4,703	12,671	39,190
Banks	n.a.	20	-5	83	934	416	3,363	3,679	6,250
Other	n.a.	1,485	2,958	7,421	6,504	4,258	-436	19,959	8,984
Middle East and North Africa	27	1,126	427	4,472	1,546	-3,431	-3,179	6,851	8,663
FDI	0	118	429	1,283	1,907	1,059	3,816	22,012	6,715
Equity	n.a.	-96	-109	-624	62	90	-241	-3,579	1,163
Banks	2	-147	91	-242	-842	1,263	-777	3,278	5,441
Other	25	1,213	15	4,056	419	-5,843	-5,978	-14,861	-4,656

Sub-Saharan Africa	27	2,923	4,422	-2,759	-3,225	3,612	-6,393	16,365	14,265
FDI	-14	534	663	1,143	1,118	4,085	10,167	19,895	15,095
Equity	4	15	2	-269	-130	2,816	-428	1,305	4,182
Banks	-89	79	-11	96	-853	-324	-2,947	2,593	-4,009
Other	126	2,294	3,767	-3,729	-3,361	-2,964	-13,184	-7,428	-1,002
Europe and Central Asia	76	3,616	-2,398	-4,698	-7,536	10,420	17,857	106,400	72,443
FDI	64	54	74	269	2,002	12,583	19,505	71,010	22,180
Equity	n.a.	n.a.	n.a.	-24	351	1,666	1,184	3,530	2,818
Banks	25	2,303	-1,141	-4,192	-3,566	4,277	2,584	26,332	34,312
Other	35	1,259	-1,332	-760	-6,323	-8,106	-5,417	5,528	13,132
Total emerging-market economies	693	26,374	31,351	3,548	76,525	117,410	82,719	334,709	571,091
FDI	569	3,849	9,328	12,530	41,207	127,306	143,973	320,905	251,631
Equity	3	-82	-98	-258	14,760	11,436	10,756	35,472	110,543
Banks	33	5,041	4,904	-7,514	1,072	-1,594	-5,480	19,964	165,663
Other	585	17,527	17,214	-1,217	19,484	-19,737	-66,531	-41,632	43,254

n.a. = not available

Note: This is an unbalanced panel, including all countries that report in a given year. Data for 2010 are annual numbers while the rest are annual averages for five-year periods. Net inflows are defined as the IMF's change in liabilities minus assets, so a negative entry means net outflow. The concept of net implicit in this table is net purchases by foreigners of assets in the defined category minus net sales by foreigners in that category. Total flows have been taken from the financial account not included elsewhere (n.i.e.) in the Balance of Payments Statistics (net sum of FDI, portfolio investment, financial derivatives, and other investment). Banks represent flows taken from a subcategory of other investment (OI), where OI is a subcomponent of the financial account. Other flows are defined as the financial account n.i.e. subtracting the corresponding net flows from FDI, equity, and banks. Other flows include portfolio debt, derivatives, deposits, loans, and trade credits. More information is available in the *International Financial Statistics* introductory chapter (page xxvii). See table 1.1 for countries covered in this table.

Source: International Monetary Fund, *International Financial Statistics*, July 2011.

shows inter alia bank lending to developing economies (a classification that includes what are now often referred to as emerging-market economies), which excludes the money that banks put into their branches and subsidiaries in these countries but includes the loans that they extend to those subsidiaries and branches. We start by examining the main characteristics of this type of capital flow, draw out some policy implications, and then analyze recent trends in bank investment in developing and emerging-market economies.

Bank Lending to Developing and Emerging-Market Economies

IMF figures for bank lending to developing and emerging-market economies are shown in table 4.6. Banks became a significant source of capital after 1974, and the biggest recipient initially was ECA, even though Communist governments were still in power. However, these flows turned around even before the debt crisis started in 1982. Flows to Latin America also were strong during the 1970s and stayed strong until the debt crisis in 1982. After that, the inflows were exaggerated by the existence of highly involuntary loans that the banks were arm-twisted into making (to serve their own collective self-interest). But such lending weakened as the 1980s progressed, and the inflow turned negative in the second half of the decade. Apart from modest inflows in the early 1990s, LAC has continued to experience net outflows in each of the five-year periods since 1990.

East Asia also emerged as a significant destination for bank lending during the 1970s. It also suffered in the wake of the debt crisis, but not as deeply as Latin America. There was a negligible outflow in the late 1980s, followed by big inflows up until the time of the Asian financial crisis in 1997, when lending fell precipitously. Initially, this sharp decline was undoubtedly because banks attempted to withdraw capital from the region, although the fact that it remained negative throughout the decade following 2000 (except for 2006) is presumably a reflection of the fact that these countries almost all built substantial current account surpluses. It is reasonable to expect this to result in state-owned enterprises stopping borrowing from foreign banks and instead of seeking loans from domestic sources.

South Asia has never absorbed large quantities of bank loans, although its borrowing became fairly substantial in some recent years. MENA has shown little increase in its overseas bank borrowing: Occasionally the flows have been sizable, especially in 2008, when the inflow to MENA was the largest to any region. Sub-Saharan Africa was a minor borrower until the mid-2000s, when its inflows increased significantly until the wake of the Lehman Brothers collapse in 2008, which led to outflows for 2009.

The real standout is ECA. The region experienced net outflows of bank lending through the later years of Communist rule and the beginning of the transition during the early 1990s, but it began to show positive inflows in the late 1990s. These became dramatically large after 2005, taking the form primarily of loans to local subsidiaries and branches of Austrian, Italian,

Table 4.6 Flow of bank funds to emerging-market economies, by region, 1970–2010 (millions of US dollars)

Region	1970–74	1975–79	1980–84	1985–89	1990–94	1995–99	2000–04
Latin America and the Caribbean	68	2,170	5,598	–3,796	737	–1,417	–2,822
East Asia and the Pacific	27	616	372	537	4,662	–5,809	–4,881
South Asia	n.a.	20	–5	83	934	416	3,363
Middle East and North Africa	2	–147	91	–242	–842	1,263	–777
Sub-Saharan Africa	–89	79	–11	96	–853	–324	–2,947
Europe and Central Asia	25	2,303	–1,141	–4,192	–3,566	4,277	2,584
Total	33	5,041	4,904	–7,514	1,072	–1,594	–5,480

Region	2005	2006	2007	2008	2009	2010
Latin America and the Caribbean	–7,875	–12,090	10,369	–948	–11,977	35,470
East Asia and the Pacific	–24,415	11,663	–24,158	–38,595	18,429	88,200
South Asia	4,257	5	8,630	6,601	–1,097	6,250
Middle East and North Africa	26	–8,737	–1,078	19,832	6,349	5,441
Sub-Saharan Africa	–1,089	–5,040	7,925	12,051	–881	–4,009
Europe and Central Asia	33,413	55,647	86,871	389	–44,658	34,312
Total	4,316	41,448	88,559	–670	–33,835	165,663

n.a. = not available

Note: This is an unbalanced panel, including all countries that report in a given year. Data for 2005–10 are annual numbers while the rest are annual averages for five-year periods. Net inflows are defined as the IMF's change in liabilities less assets, so a negative entry means net outflow. The concept of net implicit in this table is purchases by foreigners of bank assets minus sales by foreigners of bank assets. The flows of banks are a subcategory of other investment (OI), where OI is a subcategory of the financial account. More information is available in the *International Financial Statistics* introductory chapter (page xxvii). See table 1.1 for countries covered in this table.

Source: International Monetary Fund, *International Financial Statistics*, July 2011.

and Swedish banks. These outsized inflows occasioned many cautions in the precrisis period, and in fact the region experienced a much deeper recession in the wake of the global financial crisis than elsewhere in the world. For what it is worth, the fixed-exchange-rate regimes in place in these countries were maintained during the crisis.

Three dominant observations emerge from the data. The first is that there has been a strong upward trend in bank lending to developing and emerging-market economies over time. Annual inflows were around $5,000 million in the late 1970s—which itself was a dramatically larger figure than a decade earlier—and these had grown more than ten times as large during the next 25 years, by 2007. Inflation explains part of this explosion, but prices did not multiply anything like tenfold over this period.

The second observation is that bank lending to developing and emerging-market economies is highly volatile. In the words of Guillermo Calvo (1998), bank flows exhibit a series of "sudden stops." The economic ups and downs of the regions are clearly reflected in bank lending flows, including the Latin American debt crisis (starting in 1982), the Asian financial crisis (starting in 1997), Latin America's lost half-decade (1998–2002), and the Great Recession (which came to a head in 2008) and affected most severely what was then the dominant bank borrower, the ECA region. However, it is noteworthy that flows to ECA remained positive even in 2008, which contrasts with large outflows experienced by other crisis-affected regions, and this suggests that bank lending may be more stable when it goes to subsidiaries than when it goes to independent enterprises. Of course, this conclusion is subject to two caveats: No government in the region was seen as threatening the banking system, as was the Argentine government in 2002, and there was a big outflow the following year, in 2009.

The third observation is that the levels of bank lending varied dramatically by region. LAC was the largest bank borrower after lending to Communist-ruled ECA slipped, but it never regained its dominance after the debt crisis of 1982, although there has been a substantial revival of inflows in recent years. East Asia was the dominant recipient of bank loans after the debt crisis until it suffered its own crisis in 1997, and subsequent revivals of inflows have been strictly temporary. Inflows to the ECA region were fairly substantial during the prime years of Communist rule, but tailed off after 1980 until the transition was securely under way in 1995. However, ECA experienced enormous inflows after western European banks bought up large parts of the region's banking systems, and flows did not turn negative until 2009, as noted. Even South Asia and Sub-Saharan Africa have experienced substantial inflows in recent years. In contrast, inflows to MENA have shown no obvious trend, except for large inflows in 2008–09 (which could have been due to the high oil prices prevailing during that period, although it is unclear through what mechanism).

The debt crisis that began in 1982 first revealed that banks are a highly unstable source of capital. During the Asian financial crisis in 1997, this conventional wisdom was further reinforced by the reversal of bank capital flows to the region, which was in direct contrast to the flow of FDI, which held stable during the crisis years. All countries suffered from the extreme volatility in bank flows following the collapse of Lehman Brothers in 2008 (Milesi-Ferretti and Tille 2011), although the developing and emerging-market economies were less badly hit than the advanced economies (primarily because bank capital formed a much smaller share of their capital imports). However, there was a short, sharp contraction in bank flows to developing and emerging-market economies post-Lehman.

There is another risk associated with bank lending besides its proneness to sudden stops: It is almost invariably denominated in the currency of a foreign country. This means that its value increases in domestic currency terms in the event of a devaluation of the borrowing country's currency, which is normally part of the rational reaction to a sudden stop in capital flows. This feature was little noticed during the Latin American crisis, when the overwhelming problem was seen to be the absence of voluntary currency inflows, but it was regarded as a major part of the problem in the Asian financial crisis.

The likely reason for the contrast is that in the 1980s it was taken for granted that developing and emerging-market economies borrowed in creditor-country currencies, and this had changed by the 1990s. (The induced inflation of liabilities proved much less of a problem during the Great Recession, presumably because the depreciations of developing and emerging-market economies' currencies were strictly temporary.)

Bank Investment in Developing and Emerging-Market Economies

The establishment of foreign banks seems to have played a central role in the financial development of most countries except France, Germany, Great Britain, and the United States (Goldsmith 1969). Foreign bank establishment started mainly as a British initiative in the first half of the 19th century. France and Germany came into the picture in the 1880s, and the United States later still, after World War I. But the proportion of deposits held in foreign banks peaked well before 1914, and fell after World War II to such low level that the dominant theory argued that these branches (as almost all were) primarily serviced firms or people from the home countries who happened to be trading or resident in the host country (Aliber 1984). Only in recent years, as one facet of the trend toward globalization, has it been generally accepted that international banks may have a comparative advantage in providing banking services in foreign markets because of the management technology and marketing expertise they have developed in the home market (Grubel 1977). Not until the 1990s did a large number of banks recognize and seek to exploit these wider opportunities.

Financial-sector FDI (FSFDI) in developing and emerging-market economies is conventionally measured from statistics on mergers and acquisitions (M&A). According to Dietrich Domanski (2005), FSFDI rose from a modest $2.5 billion in the period 1991–95 to some $51.5 billion in 1996–2000, before stabilizing from 2001 to October 2005. (These are the latest statistics of which we are aware.) According to Milesi-Ferretti and Tille (2011, 302), on the eve of the world financial crisis in 2007 some 52 percent of foreign bank claims on developing economies took the form of lending from local affiliates of international banks.

Domanski (2005) offers some interesting contrasts in the characteristics of the inflows in the three principal regions that have hosted the most FSFDI. In Latin America, where the inflows were largest, the biggest share was from the predominantly Spanish banks that were aiming to build up a regional network. The second largest share was from large international banks that were aiming to build a global franchise. In Central and Eastern Europe the inflows were again principally from banks—most from Austria but also Italian and Swedish banks—whose ambitions were essentially regional. Only in Asia, where most inflows occurred later, was the primary motive to take advantage of favorable investment opportunities, with the primary types of inflows being either intraregional (specifically, from Hong Kong and Singapore banks) or from nonbanks, such as finance corporations and equity funds. Crises provided an important spur for the growth of FSFDI in both Latin America and Asia, while in Europe the primary motivation was the opportunities provided by privatization during the transition away from communism.

By 2004 foreign banks had already become an important part of the scenery in many developing and emerging-market economies, as the data in table 4.6 illustrate. A central normative issue is whether investment by foreign banks in developing and emerging economies can be expected to raise the efficiency of the domestic financial sector and therefore to advance the process of economic development. Earlier studies (e.g., Goldsmith 1969, McKinnon 1973, and Levine 1997) established that there were benefits of foreign financial intermediation in general, but they did not address the question of the aptness of foreign banks versus other financial intermediaries. Some of the more recent studies focus specifically on whether there are advantages in investment by foreign banks. Studies that examine the benefits of bank investment in other developed economies (e.g., Berger et al. 2000) tend to argue that on average domestic rather than foreign-based enterprises have an advantage. But even this does not get at the point of central interest here.

Perhaps the first paper to address the issue of the relative profitability of foreign-owned banks and to develop what has become a stylized fact in this area is by Asli Demirgüç-Kunt and Harry Huizinga (1999). They use bank-level data for 80 countries during the years 1988–95 to establish inter alia that foreign-owned banks have higher margins and profitability than domestic banks in developing economies, but lower margins and profitability in developed economies. A possible explanation is that foreign banks tend to be free of the credit allocation regulations that impede many domestic banks in developing economies, but tend to place a high premium on growth when operating in developed economies.

A subsequent study in which those authors participated examines a broader array of questions (Claessens, Demirgüç-Kunt, and Huizinga 2000).

This uses the same data set covering about 7,900 bank-years. They reinforce the conclusion of Demirgüç-Kunt and Huizinga (1999) that foreign banks tend to earn higher margins than domestic banks in developing economies but lower margins than domestic competitors in developed economies. The study also estimates the effect on domestic banks' performance of the entry by foreign banks. It is found that when an economy has a larger share of banks with foreign ownership there is a significant effect in reducing bank profitability, noninterest income, and overheads, which the authors interpret as showing that foreign banks' entry enhances efficiency. They find that when foreign banks have a larger ownership share of the banking system there are similar but much less pronounced effects, which they interpret as showing that the beneficial effects of foreign banks' entry occur through such mechanisms as demonstrating superior technology and encouraging better supervision, effects that depend upon the presence rather than the size of foreign banks.

Another broader study is by Felix Eschenbach, Joseph Francois, and Ludger Schuknecht (2000). They note that until the writings of Raymond Goldsmith (1969) and Ronald McKinnon (1973), the role of the financial system in the growth process was considered to be one of mobilizing savings and then passively channeling the savings to "investment." The modern view (Levine 1997) is that a good financial system can improve resource allocation over space and time. Financial markets and intermediaries can pool risks and develop tradable financial instruments that promote investment in growth-enhancing but risky activities. They enable individual savers and/or investors to hold diversified, less risky, and more liquid portfolios while still providing finance to high-risk enterprises. Financial intermediaries generate information about the relative merits of different investment opportunities and monitor the managers of enterprises.

Finally, banks facilitate the exchange of goods and services through trade financing and the maintenance of payments systems. These functions may promote growth either by increasing the quantity of capital accumulation or by allocating capital to more productive enterprises.

Eschenbach, Francois, and Schuknecht (2000) also conduct a standard cross-country growth regression designed to explore the benefits of trade in financial services. It turns out that open (and therefore presumably more competitive) financial sectors are one of the variables most strongly correlated with growth, which leads them to conclude that financial services trade enhances growth. It is true that the focus is on trade in financial services in general rather than on investment in banks in particular, but it is also true that foreign banks are in practice the preeminent form of trade in financial services. However, their analysis does not note or make allowance for the possibility of reverse causation.

Adolfo Barajas, Natalia Salazar, and Roberto Steiner (2000) study the effect of liberalizing the entry of foreign-owned financial institutions in Colombia in the early 1990s. After tracing the fluctuations of Colombian policy on this issue, they run a panel regression explaining intermediation spreads as a function of a number of variables: microeconomic indicators, banking sector dummies, liberalization and entry variables, and measures of macroeconomic conditions. They observe:

> ...the results give overwhelming evidence of a beneficial impact of foreign entry. Whether market or number penetration indicators...are used, foreign entry appears to have a significant effect in lowering spreads, reducing nonfinancial costs, and improving loan quality (reducing the percentage of nonperforming loans) in the banking system. (p. 376)

This preliminary analysis was supplemented by three additional regressions, one that acknowledges the possibility that other liberalization effects may have occurred during the period in which foreign entry occurred, and two in which the effects on domestic and foreign banks were considered separately. The authors conclude that the preliminary evidence had tended to overstate the benefits of foreign entry since other aspects were also important—notably increased entry of domestic banks, capital account liberalization, and improved regulation and supervision—but that foreign bank entry continued to play a significant role.

A study of the impact of foreign bank entry on the Turkish banking system was conducted by Cevdet Denizer (2000). Turkey had only four foreign banks when it started to liberalize its economic policy after the crisis of 1980, but the number had increased to 23 a decade later, before a few of them were squeezed out in the 1990s. Regression analysis in this study suggests that foreign banks enhance competition and reduce domestic bank profitability. The results are even more significant when the return on assets is adjusted for inflation. There are also indications that foreign bank entry had a positive impact on sundry qualitative dimensions of financial sector development.

Jennifer Crystal, Gerard Dages, and Linda Goldberg (2001) ask whether Latin America benefited from the wave of foreign takeovers of their banks in the 1990s. They compare the performance of foreign banks with domestically owned private and state-owned banks in the seven large economies in the region. They show that the BFSRs (Moody's Bank Financial Strength Ratings) of foreign-owned banks improved marginally in the five years following foreign acquisition and that the improvement was somewhat greater when compared to a cohort of domestic banks. Three countries—Argentina, Chile, and Colombia—had data that permit more extensive comparisons. No dramatic differences are revealed, except for inferior performance by state-owned banks, but foreign banks manifested consistently faster average loan growth than domestic privately owned banks, higher loan provisioning, higher average recoveries, higher risk-based capital ratios, but similar or weaker overall profitability. The authors argue that the high provisioning levels argue against the "cherry-picking" theory (that foreign banks specialize in lending to less-risky borrowers, forcing domestic lenders to accept greater risk). They clearly regard their findings as consistent with the view that foreign banks have access to superior technology, which they employ primarily to pursue less risky lending.

Donald Mathieson and Jorge Roldós (2001) give a broad sketch of foreign banks' activity in emerging-market economies, which notably increased during the 1990s. They find that higher profitability tended to increase foreign bank investment, as did a high proportion of nonperforming loans in domestic banks, a recent banking crisis, and better macroeconomic conditions. They outline arguments that have become standard in discussions about the potential costs and benefits of the role of foreign banks: the potential for broad improvements in banking technology versus the risk that foreign banks cherry-pick the best debtors; the potential stability accruing from foreign banks being less vulnerable to shocks in the host country; the ability of depositors to shift deposits to foreign banks and so obviate a run on the currency in times of crisis; the potential danger that foreign banks will provoke domestic institutions into gambling for survival; foreign banks' ability to cut and run; and the potential danger that they escape supervision from both home and host authorities. In fact, the paper anticipates what occurred during the recent crisis in noting that foreign banks could use over-the-counter derivative products to evade effective supervision, but the remedy they offer is that supervisors learn all about these products rather than effectively ban their use. There is a rather inconclusive discussion of whether foreign banks worsen the problem of having banks that are too big to fail.

A subsequent chapter in the same book by Michael Pomerleano and George J. Vojta (2001) expresses none of the doubts raised by Mathieson and Roldós (2001) about the benefits to be derived from the presence of foreign banks. Pomerleano and Vojta describe strategies pursued by foreign versus domestic banks, finding that some banks still maintain foreign operations for the benefit of their compatriots running international companies, but that most either target the top end of the commercial banking market or were primarily involved in investment banking. Some domestic banks emulate the foreigners, but most are either refocusing their role on the corporate sector or concentrating on retail establishments and small and medium enterprises (SMEs). They find that foreign banks have a particular advantage in products that require a global platform, like foreign exchange transactions and syndicated lending, while domestic banks have an advantage in products like funding and know-how that require local capabilities. Their conclusion starts with this endorsement of foreign banks:

> The evidence presented in this paper confirms that domestic policymakers should welcome foreign banks. The current trend in banking is the consolidation of global financial services in the hands of about twenty very large global players. These institutions can afford the greatest range of products and services, make the largest investments, manage the most information, and rationalize costs and risks most efficiently. They offer an unsurpassed level.... (p. 91)

George Clarke, Robert Cull, and Martinez Peria (2001) report the results of a large-scale survey of users of bank credit. They find that foreign banks do grant a lower percentage of their loans to SMEs, but that SMEs do not suffer by the entry of foreign banks because this is more than offset by two contrary factors: the improvement of the banking system as a whole by the increased competition and improved stability and efficiency resulting from the entry of foreign banks and the diversion of lending of the other banks to SMEs. Clarke, Cull, and Peria conclude, however, that large enterprises benefit more than smaller enterprises by the entry of foreign banks.

Atif Mian (2003) finds that domestic and private banks tend to have similar profitability despite their very different strengths, and credits this in particular to the ability of foreign banks to lower their deposit costs by drawing on the liquidity of home country headquarters. He argues that the distance between management and the local culture restricts foreign banks' lending to those that can provide "hard information," whereas the rate of return tends to be higher for lenders who rely on "soft information," which is generally acceptable only to those lenders who come from the same culture.

The Inter-American Development Bank (IDB) analyzed commercial bank lending in Latin America (IDB 2004). In fact, this analysis was the basis for the IDB's subsequent *Economic and Social Progress Report* (IDB 2005), which specifically examined the increase of foreign banking activity in the region. It finds evidence that foreign bank entry expands credit (though disproportionately to large firms), that foreign banks tend to be more efficient than domestic banks, and that they have lower net intermediation margins (which they can afford because they have lower overhead costs).

However, the study also finds that foreign banks may exploit their superior exit strategies in case of problems arising from shocks to the economy in general. They also may transmit shocks originating in their home countries to the host countries. On the other hand, if the shocks arose from a decline in deposits in the host country, including a confidence-inspired run on deposits, foreign banks are less apt to cut loans than domestic banks. This is partly because they may be able to draw on foreign resources and partly because a run on deposits is less likely to include foreign banks because depositors tend to have greater confidence in them.

Alejandro Micco, Ugo Panizza, and Mónica Yañez (2004) built a data set on bank ownership and performance with about 50,000 observations for 119 countries over the period 1995–2002. Their objective was to have a more comprehensive dataset to retest several propositions suggested in the literature. By simply comparing median values, they confirm that foreign banks tend to be more profitable than privately owned domestic competitors in developing economies but less profitable in developed economies.

However, they also conclude that while this was true in general, it was not true for all regions: In particular, it was not true for Latin America (contradicting a finding of IDB 2005). They conclude that foreign banks are more efficient than domestic privately owned banks in terms of overhead costs, employment, and the number of branches. They confirm the results of Demirgüç-Kunt and Huizinga (1999) on the impact of privatization and the switch to foreign ownership, showing that foreign banks tend to acquire domestic banks that previously had low profitability. However, they did not replicate the results of Claessens, Demirgüç-Kunt and Huizinga (2001) regarding the beneficial impact of foreign bank entry on the efficiency of the domestic banking system.

John Bonin, Iftekhar Hasan, and Paul Wachtel (2005) examine the impact of ownership on efficiency for 11 transition countries over the period 1996–2000. They find that banks that are foreign owned are more cost-efficient and provide better service.

An authoritative summary of foreign bank investment as of the mid-2000s is provided by Ramon Moreno and Augustin Villar (2005), from the Bank for International Settlements (BIS). They take for granted that foreign banks offer important attractions to emerging-market economies on account of efficiency and competitiveness. They note that there had been a strategic shift by foreign banks away from concentrating on corporate clients from their home countries toward seeking to exploit business opportunities in the local markets. They also note the tendency of such banks to replace on-lending of home-office funds denominated in dollars with local-currency lending by local affiliates (although they note that this implies a reduction in the foreign capital brought in by the banks). They find sharp regional differences in the degree of foreign penetration, which was then substantial in Latin America and Central Europe and smaller in Asia. They argue that foreign banks can be of particular value during banking crises, since they are diversified rather than exposed only to the host country. They cite empirical studies undertaken in the BIS that confirm that foreign banks tend to play a stabilizing role and seem puzzled at findings that foreign banks had not played a stabilizing role in Argentina's crisis of 2001. However, they raise four major sources of potential risks. First, when foreign banks are not supervised by the host country, there is less information for the local supervisor. Second, shocks to the home country can be transmitted to the host country (though they argue that this vulnerability is comparable to having the host-country borrowers indebted for an equal sum through independent bank transactions with the home country). Third, banks may not be penalized for extending foreign-currency loans to clients in the nontradable sector. Finally, and rather surprisingly, since it goes against most other published material, they worry that foreign bank entry might reduce competition.

Ralph De Haas and Iman Van Lelyveld (2006) empirically investigate whether foreign-owned banks react differently from domestic banks to cyclical events and banking crises in Central and Eastern Europe. Their panel dataset covers 250 banks for the period 1993–2000. They find some significant differences, at least for greenfield foreign banks. Domestic banks contracted their credit base during crises, whereas greenfield foreign banks did not. There is a significant negative relationship between home-country economic growth and the credit granted by foreign greenfields in the host countries.

Mariassunta Gianetti and Steven Ongena (2009) study the impact of foreign bank entry on small and young firms. They use a panel of 60,000 firm-year observations in Eastern European economies to assess the differential impact of foreign bank lending on firm growth and financing. They find that in general foreign lending stimulates the growth of firms' sales and assets and their use of financial debt. This effect is attenuated for small firms but magnified for young firms.

Juan Cárdenas, Juan Pablo Graf, and Pascual O'Dogherty (2003), from the Banco de México, accept that foreign banks bring important benefits by virtue of efficiency gains from new technologies, increased competition, reduced exposure to stresses originating in the host country, and less susceptibility to connected lending. On the other hand, they consider them more prone to cut and run in times of adversity because they have both more foreign investment opportunities and fewer problems in unloading their financial investments than local stockholders, which may make the host economy more vulnerable to events in the rest of the world.[10] Furthermore, although foreign-owned banks empirically enjoy higher credit ratings, it is not a given that foreign ownership guarantees support—for example, several foreign banks did not stand behind their Argentinean subsidiaries during the 2001 crisis. Many global financial firms increasingly concentrate operations (such as risk management) that were formerly the responsibility of subsidiaries into global hubs like London in order to take advantage of scale economies and lax regulation. This leaves local subsidiaries subject to wide fluctuations in their profit and loss positions. Similarly, country credit risks are concentrated in the country where they originate, which results in local subsidiaries losing the potential advantages of holding a geographically more diversified portfolio. Again, banks in emerging-market economies that are taken over have their own foreign funding subsidiaries closed, which increases the risks that the subsidiary will face wide fluctuations in its earnings and increases its dependence on funding by the parent. Unless the subsidiary is required by law to place its own interests first, its interests will likely be considered secondary to those of the parent. The sale of a locally owned bank to foreign owners also may result in local delisting and therefore lead to an important loss of information to the local supervisory authorities and the local capital market. In sum, there are serious costs to foreign bank ownership, some but not all of which can be mitigated by such measures as a legal requirement that subsidiaries put their own interests first or a prohibition of 100 percent foreign ownership combined with a requirement that the local shares of the jointly owned subsidiary be quoted on the local stock exchange.

What can one conclude from these studies? First, the overwhelming weight of evidence seems to be that foreign entry tends to increase the effi-

---

10. This involves a comparison with local banks; they concurred that offshore lending is more volatile than onshore lending by international banks, though this diminished volatility is bought at the cost of less international borrowing.

ciency of the domestic financial sector, essentially by importing improved banking technology, in emerging-market economies (though not in industrialized economies and, as one study suggests, possibly not in Latin America). Similarly, there seems to be wide (though not unanimous) agreement that foreign bank ownership increases competition. The charge that foreign-owned banks cherry-pick the best borrowers seems to have been effectively refuted by the finding that although large enterprises have the most enhanced access to credit (they are the cherries), the SMEs also gain by virtue of general gains and the diversion of lending toward them by domestic banks (Clarke, Cull, and Peria 2001). There seems to be general agreement that foreign banks are less vulnerable to domestic shocks and that the ability to shift deposits to foreign-owned domestic banks in the event of a crisis makes the consequences of a crisis less severe. Domestic and foreign banks may be equally profitable, although this is likely a result of the superiority of the foreign banks in using hard information in lending decisions, which roughly offsets the cultural advantages of domestic banks which are better able to exploit soft information.

But these observations leave a series of potential risks that have not been decisively refuted. First, a premature liberalization of foreign bank entry may provoke marginal domestic institutions to gamble for survival. Second, foreign banks can cut and run when conditions turn adverse (although there is no proper study of whether the tendency to cut and run is worse if a foreign bank has established a bank than if it is lending an equivalent sum on the open market). Third, therefore, foreign banks may constitute a channel for contagion. Fourth, foreign-owned banks may escape effective supervision, either because they don't supply information to local authorities when a 100 percent foreign takeover occurs or because they deal in unsupervised instruments like over-the-counter derivatives.

5

Conclusion: A New International Pact on Capital Flows

Capital controls are making a comeback. This is not necessarily bad news, because there are situations when such controls can be beneficial. However, in some cases, capital controls are more likely to be distortive than corrective. The resurgence in the use of capital controls therefore should compel the international community to more systematically coordinate their use in ways that lead to better national policy and international regulations.

Need for Symmetric Rules on the Use of Capital Controls

There are three key factors (a combination of theory and empirics) that should be addressed by any effort to develop symmetric international rules on the use of capital controls. Each of these three is analyzed in depth in this study.

First, international financial integration and openness to capital (especially debt) flows provide little if anything by way of boosting long-run growth. This is suggested in the academic literature and overwhelmingly substantiated by our research as reported in chapter 3.

Second, as argued in chapter 2, there is a good case to be made for using certain types of controls, notably prudential and countercyclical capital controls that can be effective in smoothing booms and busts in capital flows to developing and emerging-market economies. In fact, this has been the impetus for the recent implementation of such controls by a number of countries (notably Brazil, as described in chapter 1).

We find that capital controls can be part of the menu of options to be deployed in the last resort against incipient asset price bubbles, a position that the International Monetary Fund (IMF), long an opponent of the use of such controls, has recently endorsed. However, our findings go further:

Properly designed capital controls may even be effective as a regular instrument of economic policy and may be warranted in other situations that are not strictly related to capital booms and busts. One such situation would be when a country runs a structural current account deficit; maintaining capital controls can be a precautionary measure to prevent overvaluation of a currency (and thus penalize the tradable goods sector). India may be an example of this type of situation. Another situation in which capital controls may be warranted is when a country seeks to protect a fragile home banking sector from the destabilizing entry of foreign banks (or from other forms of capital inflows).

The third key factor to be addressed in any international effort to regulate the use of capital controls is raised by the recent standoff between the United States and China and the acrimonious discussions about the value of the Chinese currency, the yuan. As this demonstrates, a country can use capital controls to sustain an undervalued exchange rate as an instrument of mercantilism with beggar-thy-neighbor effects on its trading partners and hence as a tool to prevent the exchange rate adjustments that are necessary to rebalance the global economy. China has used capital account restrictions combined with exchange market intervention to maintain a persistent real exchange rate undervaluation that is economically equivalent to a tariff on imports and a subsidy for exports.

The trade effects of China's policy highlight the close connections between capital flows and trade flows and raise the question of whether these links should be considered in the design of any international rules that affect either. In reality, there is an asymmetry between the international regulation of trade in goods and trade in financial assets and capital flows. Under the World Trade Organization (WTO) and its predecessor, the General Agreement on Tariffs and Trade (GATT), international rules were promulgated to promote free trade in goods. In contrast, trade in financial assets and capital flows has been largely left to the discretion of individual countries, and this is reflected most saliently in the fact that the IMF has no jurisdiction over how its member countries manage their capital account.[1]

The challenge in designing international rules on capital controls is to design a system that permits the use of controls that are welfare-improving but prevents or restricts the use of those that are not.

---

1. The exceptions, of course, are flows of certain types of capital—such as foreign direct investment (FDI) in services, which is regulated under the General Agreement on Trade in Services (GATS). Also, the lacunae that we have identified relate to worldwide rules because under bilateral and multilateral agreements both goods and capital may be regulated. For example, many free trade agreements recently signed by the United States—with Chile and Singapore, for example—prohibit the imposition of capital controls even for prudential reasons. Also, the Organization for Economic Cooperation and Development (OECD) has long promoted free capital mobility.

Three Alternative Approaches to International Cooperation on Capital Flows

We consider three alternative approaches to international cooperation—in ascending order of ambition—that take account of the three key factors discussed above. We discuss the pros and cons of each option.

Maintain the Status Quo

There may not be a need for new levels of international cooperation, given the desirability of using countercyclical restrictions to address booms and busts or the benefits of maintaining other restrictions to avoid macroeconomic instability and overvaluation. After all, the status quo is permissive in providing individual countries the policy space to impose any kind of macroprudential capital account restrictions. And, indeed, this freedom has been recently exploited by a number of countries, including Brazil, that have implemented such measures. Why build a new cooperative apparatus when the status quo works well?

The case for cooperation, in our view, is twofold, stemming ironically from the fact that the status quo is not permissive enough in some ways and is too permissive in others. Because the overall international economic environment favors openness, there is a stigma attendant to any policy measures that depart from such openness. Therefore, the status quo can be considered to place de facto limits on the freedom of countries to effectively use capital controls. This is evident in the fact that, in late 2009, Brazil imposed only very weak restrictions on capital inflows in order to avoid rattling the markets and ended up incurring the stigma of being market-unfriendly without effectively addressing the inflow problem. Brazil arguably should have imposed higher taxes (as it did eventually) at the outset to stem the flood of capital. Enhanced cooperation and internationally agreed rules could sanction the use by countries of the most appropriate and effective measures.

At the same time, the lack of internationally agreed rules does, on occasion, tempt countries to impose or maintain measures that are in fact damaging. The outstanding contemporary case is China, which is breaking no international rules in using capital controls as an instrument for maintaining an undervalued currency. In fact, the status quo has been characterized by mercantilism, global imbalances, and the prospect of currency and trade wars.

Develop a Code of Conduct for Nondistortive Capital Measures

A second alternative is for the IMF to devise a code of good conduct on nondistortive capital restrictions that countries can follow if they are afflicted by problems associated with inflows. This approach would have the overarching merit of drawing out and addressing one of the central lessons from the recent financial crisis, namely that distortive capital controls can magnify the loss of welfare for individual countries and for the global economy in a crisis.

An international code of conduct might be inadequate or ineffective, however, if it were limited to blessing the use of macroprudential restrictions. The recent crisis presents a unique opportunity to revisit issues related to international capital flows, and this opportunity would be wasted if it were not used to deal also with the other major lesson from the crisis, namely that global imbalances and undervalued exchange rates are exerting a significant drag on global growth. There is an opportunity to rectify the asymmetry between the international rules for trade in goods and trade in capital, as we discuss below.

The politics involved in bargaining over new international rules may in fact be made a little less difficult by a more ambitious approach that also addresses issues related to the imbalances between countries with capital account surpluses and those with deficits. Specifically, new rules on the use of macroprudential and other nondistortive capital measures would be beneficial to developing and emerging-market economies, and in return they may be willing to give up some policy space to reach agreement on rules governing the use of capital controls to support currency undervaluation. Whether this type of bargain would be sufficient to lead to a broad agreement remains distinctly unclear, but an ambitious approach at least opens up some additional scope for negotiation between the major players.

Given these considerations, we favor a third and much more ambitious approach.

Undertake Ambitious International Oversight of Capital Controls

The asymmetry between the international rules governing capital flows and the rules governing trade in goods are problematic, especially in the current global economic environment, and can in fact threaten the global free trade regime.[2] It therefore seems natural to move toward greater symmetry in the treatment of trade in goods and trade in financial assets and capital.

We propose moving in the direction of symmetry, but remain mindful of the evidence. Since free trade in capital does not have the same long-run growth effects as free trade in goods, we propose that all countries retain a certain degree of discretion in their ability to use capital controls. Even under the GATT/WTO system, countries have always been able to implement tariffs, and so allowing a measure of capital account protection would not be particularly generous or distortive.

However, as under the rules governing trade in goods, we strongly favor transparent, price-based measures rather than quantitative measures whenever possible. This will allow the international community to more easily assess the impact of controls and limit any potential distortionary effects. Administrative controls should be allowed only if it is impossible or difficult to replace them

---

2. This asymmetry may have been less of an issue when exchange rates were managed collectively, as under the original Bretton Woods system, or when the world was in full employment, as before the Great Recession.

with market-based measures (for example, concerning measures to restrict the entry of foreign banks for prudential reasons). As under the rules governing trade in goods, countries would be allowed discretion in determining the magnitude of their administrative controls, but would be required to "bind" them—that is, they would not be allowed to implement administrative controls beyond those currently in place.

We also propose that any international rules allow countries to impose capital controls for prudential reasons, but that they should be required to make a plausible case for them. The IMF should develop the jurisprudence on the appropriate circumstances for the use of prudential measures, including the kind of measures that can be imposed, the types of flows that can be targeted, and the acceptable magnitude of any controls. We recognize that making such judgments may be difficult in practice, in particular because they will depend on the existing global conditions and not only on the features of the particular measures taken by individual countries. The IMF could pay particular attention to the impact of spillovers in third countries to deem whether controls should be considered distortive in particular circumstances.

Leaving this type of room for discretion would be symmetric with rules on trade in goods, which allow contingent protection measures as part of safeguard measures, countervailing duties, and antidumping actions. These contingent actions are considered safety valves that allow the underlying liberalization agenda to move forward by guaranteeing some relief against the unavoidable political pressures when conditions turn bad in a particular economy or in particular sectors. By analogy, if countries have the assurance that they can legitimately and without stigma impose prudential capital controls, they may move faster to eliminate the use of controls that are more structural.

We therefore propose the following two principles for the international oversight of capital controls. First, capital controls should be market based, and whenever feasible they should take the form of a tax on capital flows.[3] Second, administrative controls could be maintained if a prudential justification can be given, but they should otherwise be phased out over time and on an accelerated schedule for large, systemically important countries that have a greater potential to inflict negative externalities and for countries for which the evidence of exchange rate distortion is particularly strong.

What level of taxes should be permissible on capital controls? One option is to set a limit on the maximum tax, say 15 percent. As shown in chapter 2, 15 percent is the optimal level of prudential taxation found by calibrated models. Furthermore, this level would ensure that, if the controls prove distor-

---

3. This is important to give the international community an indication about the size of the maximum distortion induced by capital controls. Domestic prudential regulation is partly quantitative, perhaps because financial regulators cannot be sure how financial flows will respond to changes in the price of risk. Given that quantitative measures will continue to be used in domestic prudential regulation, we argue that capital controls should normally be limited to price-based instruments.

tive rather than corrective, the extent of the distortion would be relatively limited. As explained in chapter 2, the maximum impact of controls on the real exchange rate is of the same order of magnitude as the size of the tax, and so this would ensure that any distortion of real exchange rates would be limited to 15 percent or less.

How should administrative capital controls be phased out? There are several possibilities. As for trade in goods, there could be a timetable for phasing out existing controls to be set either unilaterally by some international regulatory authority or as part of negotiations. If this is considered too weak, there could be an extra requirement that the phaseout be more expeditious for larger countries that have greater capacity to inflict negative externalities on other countries or for countries that also seem to distort their real exchange rate through other policies (such as reserve accumulation).

There are pros and cons to these proposals. On the one hand, a purist view is that any rules should be uniformly applicable. But this would mean that small, economically vulnerable developing economies would be required to dismantle all administrative controls unless there are prudential reasons to justify them, which could open them to significant economic volatility. On the other hand, pragmatism dictates that the rules be more stringent for countries that are more systemically important. There is a precedent for the latter under the WTO rules, which are more stringent on the use of export subsidies by countries that trade more.

Any new rules should be embodied in an international code of good practices developed under the auspices of the IMF. In addition, the IMF could be given jurisdiction over capital account policies (a question previously debated in the 1990s, but in a very different context). Because the new rules would encompass both trade in goods and trade in financial assets, the new regime should be accompanied by a system for institutional cooperation between the IMF and the WTO, as proposed by Aaditya Mattoo and Arvind Subramanian (2008).

Any rules implemented to discourage and phase out the use of distortive capital controls can be complementary to rules directed at disciplining undervalued exchange rates, as proposed by Mattoo and Subramanian (2008). For example, there may be a situation where a country is offered the choice of either directly eliminating a currency undervaluation (for example, by refraining from intervening in foreign exchange markets or accepting supervision of its target rate) or phasing out existing restrictions on capital flows.

Fostering International Cooperation to Develop International Rules

It may be relatively easy to prescribe a set of ideal rules, but it is much more difficult to propose just how these rules can be negotiated through a cooperative international effort. In particular, what would be the incentives for those who regard themselves as potential losers—the structural undervaluers such as

China—to participate in such an agreement? There is a fairly broad menu of options—both carrots and sticks—available to induce the cooperation of individual countries because the interrelationships and symmetries between trade in goods and trade in capital allow for instruments and actions that target activity in both realms. Since China is likely to be a critical player in the success of any potential agreement, the carrots and sticks that affect it are particularly relevant.

One advantage of a collective multilateral effort to design international rules is that the wide range of affected countries can collectively bring pressure on China to participate. Recent unilateral efforts in this regard, particularly by the United States, have been largely unsuccessful. Also, an agreement on universal rules would avoid specifically targeting China (or any other country) and all countries would therefore find it more politically palatable to participate.

Some of the carrots available in the trade arena include granting China the status of a market economy under WTO rules, which would make it less vulnerable to arbitrary unilateral action—especially antidumping duties—by its trading partners (Messerlin 2004). At the moment, the restrictions on such actions are less stringent when the target is a nonmarket economy.[4]

Clear rules on sovereign wealth fund (SWF) investments could be another inducement for China to cooperate. These could take the form of securing investment opportunities for China's SWFs in an environment where Chinese investments could otherwise increasingly be subject to national regulations with a protectionist slant. China's huge stockpile of foreign reserves is not likely to be eliminated any time soon, which means that the Chinese government will be a foreign investor for some considerable time, and guaranteeing an outlet for such investment could be an important carrot for China (and also for oil-exporting countries). The nature of other potential carrots in this area is spelled out in Mattoo and Subramanian (2008).

One of the potential sticks related to trade in goods is the imposition of tariffs on countries that do not agree to bring their capital account restrictions in line with new rules. This was one aspect of legislation introduced in 2010 in the US Senate by Senators Charles Schumer and Lindsey Graham, which included the imposition of a 27.5 percent tariff on Chinese imports. More recently, the House of Representatives passed legislation that would

---

4. In order to establish that dumping is occurring, a firm's home and export prices are compared. This is the normal procedure for market economies, where home prices are assumed to reflect the true costs of production. If the overseas prices are below domestic prices, it is likely that they will be found to be "less than fair value," creating a presumption of dumping. In the case of China, because home prices are presumed to be distorted, investigators have the freedom to find comparable firms in third countries, say, India or Japan, to determine the "real" market costs of producing those goods. If the Chinese firm is selling its exports for less than the Indian or Japanese firms' costs, then it can be found to be selling goods for less than fair value. The key point is that antidumping investigators have such wide discretion in choosing comparable firms in other countries that it becomes easier to establish dumping and hence take action against Chinese imports.

allow undervalued exchange rates to be treated as export subsidies and hence subject to countervailing duties. Such linking of capital account policies and trade policies makes a lot of sense since, as we argue in chapter 2, it is possible to achieve with capital account restrictions exactly the same impacts on trade as through the imposition of tariffs on imports.

Sticks related to trade in assets could take the form of a broad reciprocity requirement,[5] whereby capital-importing countries limit sales of their public debt to include only official institutions from countries in which they themselves are allowed to buy and hold public debt. For example, instead of "moral suasion," the Chinese authorities would not be allowed to buy US Treasury bills or Japanese government bonds unless and until they allow foreigners to buy domestic Chinese debt.[6] A variant of this—a generalization of the proposal by Joseph Gagnon and Gary Hufbauer (2011)—is that a country could impose a tax on the holding of foreign assets by any countries that fail to sign on to the new rules (which is easily justified in terms of reciprocity). One advantage of this type of measure is that such countries would not violate existing multilateral rules, because there are none.[7]

Of course, it remains to be seen whether any of these carrots and sticks might be successful in inducing China to cooperate, but they are certainly worth a try, and cannot be worse than the status quo, which has been characterized by mercantilism, global imbalances, and the prospect of currency and trade wars.

As this study makes clear, the free international mobility of capital should not be considered the ideal toward which all countries world should aspire. There is only weak evidence that free capital mobility promotes long-run growth, but there is a strong case to be made for the use of capital controls to address short-run volatility. At the same time, it is appropriate to harmonize the regulations governing the international flow of capital in order to eliminate the asymmetry between the nonexistent rules governing trade in financial assets and the strong international regime promoting and governing trade in goods.

John Maynard Keynes, even in his most protectionist incarnation, famously tried to distinguish between the optimal degrees of insularity in the

---

5. See C. Fred Bergsten, "We Can Fight Fire with Fire on the Renminbi," *Financial Times,* October 4, 2010. See also Daniel Gros, "How to Avoid Trade War: A Reciprocity Requirement," VoxEU, October 8, 2010, www.voxeu.org.

6. The Chinese government debt is relatively small, and so this requirement would have to be extended to other forms of debt such as the central bank's sterilization bonds or even to private debt.

7. One obvious objection to this proposal would be that China could buy US bonds through intermediaries. But intermediaries would put themselves at considerable risk of enforcement action under existing anti-money-laundering rules. Given the sums involved, it would be hard to dissemble such operations. A more substantial objection is that the Chinese authorities could avoid the pressure by purchasing private instead of official debt.

domains of goods and capital: Let goods be home-spun as far as possible, he said, adding that "above all, let finance be primarily national" (Keynes 1933). Such a nationalistic approach has clearly been made obsolete, with trade in both goods and financial assets highly globalized, but it may still be preferable to keep trade in goods more open and unfettered than trade in capital and financial assets. Even so, there is no case at all to maintain the status quo of regulating the former and not the latter. Rules to deal jointly with trade in goods and trade in financial assets are long overdue.

References

Abiad, Abdul, Enrica Detragiache, and Thierry Tressel. 2008. *A New Database of Financial Reforms.* IMF Working Paper 08/266 (December). Washington: International Monetary Fund.

Acemoglu, Daron, Simon Johnson, James Robinson, and Pierre Yared. 2008. Income and Democracy. *American Economic Review* 98, no. 3 (June): 808–42.

Aghion, Philippe, Philippe Bacchetta, and Abhijit Banerjee. 2004. A Corporate Balance-Sheet Approach to Currency Crises. *Journal of Economic Theory* 119, no. 1 (November): 6–30.

Aitken, Brian, and Ann Harrison. 1999. Do Domestic Firms Benefit from Direct Foreign Investment? Evidence from Venezuela. *American Economic Review* 89, no. 3 (June): 605–18.

Aizenman, Joshua. 2011. Hoarding International Reserves versus a Pigouvian Tax-Cum-Subsidy Scheme: Reflections on the Deleveraging Crisis of 2008-9, and a Cost Benefit Analysis. *Journal of Economic Dynamics and Control* 35, no. 9: 1502–13.

Aizenman, Joshua, Brian Pinto, and Artur Radziwill. 2007. Sources for Financing Domestic Capital—Is Foreign Saving a Viable Option for Developing Countries? *Journal of International Money and Finance* 26, no. 5 (September): 682–702.

Akira, Ariyoshi, Karl Habermeier, Bernard Laurens, Inci Ötker-Robe, Jorge Iván Canales-Kriljenko, and Andrei Kirilenko. 2000. *Capital Controls: Country Experiences with Their Use and Liberalization.* Occasional Paper 190. Washington: International Monetary Fund.

Alfaro, Laura, Areendam Chanda, Sebnem Kalemli-Ozcan, and Selin Sayek. 2004. FDI and Economic Growth: The Role of Local Financial Markets. *Journal of International Economics* 64, no. 1 (October): 89–112.

Alfaro, Laura, Sebnem Kalemli-Ozcan, and Vadym Volosovych. 2007. Capital Flows in a Globalized World: The Role of Policies and Institutions. In *Capital Controls and Capital Flows in Emerging Economies: Policies, Practices and Consequences*, ed. Sebastian Edwards. Chicago: University of Chicago Press for National Bureau of Economic Research.

Aliber, Robert. 1984. International Banking: A Survey. *Journal of Money, Credit, and Banking* 16, no. 4 (November): 661–78.

Arteta, Carlos, Barry Eichengreen, and Charles Wyplosz. 2001. *When Does Capital Account Liberalization Help More than It Hurts?* NBER Working Paper 8414 (August). Cambridge, MA: National Bureau of Economic Research.

Barajas, Adolfo, Natalia Salazar, and Roberto Steiner. 2000. Foreign Investment in Colombia's Financial Sector. In *The Internationalization of Financial Services: Issues and Lessons for Developing Countries*, ed. Stijn Claessens and Marion Jansen. London: Kluwer Law International.

Barro, Robert, and Xavier Sala-i-Martin. 2003. *Economic Growth*, 2d ed. Cambridge, MA: MIT Press.

Barro, Robert, and Jong-Wha Lee. 2010. *A New Data Set of Educational Attainment*. NBER Working Paper 15 902. Cambridge, MA: National Bureau of Economic Research.

Bekaert, Geert, and Campbell Harvey. 2000. Foreign Speculators and Emerging Equity Markets. *Journal of Finance* 55, no. 2 (April): 565–613.

Bekaert, Geert, Campbell Harvey, and Christian Lundblad. 2005. Does Financial Liberalization Spur Growth? *Journal of Financial Economics* 77, no. 1 (July): 3–55.

Bekaert, Geert, Campbell Harvey, and Christian Lundblad. 2006. Growth Volatility and Financial Liberalization. *Journal of International Money and Finance* 25, no. 3 (April): 370–403.

Berger, Allen, Robert DeYoung, Hesna Genay, and Gregory Udell. 2000. *Globalization of Financial Institutions: Evidence from Cross-Border Banking Performance*. Finance and Economics Discussion Series 2000-04. Washington: Board of Governors of the Federal Reserve System.

Bhagwati, Jagdish. 1998. The Capital Myth: The Difference between Trade in Goods and in Dollars. *Foreign Affairs* (May/June).

Bianchi, Javier. 2011. Overborrowing and Systemic Externalities in the Business Cycle. *American Economic Review* 101, no. 7: 3400–20.

Blalock, Garrick, and Paul Gertler. 2008. Welfare Gains from Foreign Direct Investment through Technology Transfer to Local Suppliers. *Journal of International Economics* 74, no. 2 (March): 402–21.

Blanchard, Olivier, and Gian Maria Milesi-Ferretti. 2009. *Global Imbalances: In Midstream?* IMF Staff Position Note 09/29. Washington: International Monetary Fund.

Bonin, John, Iftekhar Hasan, and Paul Wachtel. 2005. Bank Performance, Efficiency, and Ownership in Transition Countries. *Journal of Banking and Finance* 29, no. 1 (January): 31–53.

Borensztein, Eduardo, Jose De Gregorio, and Jong-Wha Lee. 1998. How Does Foreign Direct Investment Affect Economic Growth? *Journal of International Economics* 45, no. 1 (June): 115–35.

Caballero, Ricardo J., Emmanuel Farhi, and Pierre-Olivier Gourinchas. 2008. An Equilibrium Model of "Global Imbalances" and Low Interest Rates. *American Economic Review* 98, no. 1: 358–93.

Caballero, Ricardo J., and Guido Lorenzoni. 2009. *Persistent Appreciations and Overshooting: A Normative Analysis*. Revised version of NBER Working Paper 13077. Cambridge, MA: MIT and National Bureau of Economic Research. Available at http://econ-www.mit.edu/files/4454.

Calvo, Guillermo. 1998. Capital Flows and Capital Market Crises: The Economics of Sudden Stops. *Journal of Applied Economics* no. 1: 35–54.

Cárdenas, Juan, Juan Pablo Graf, and Pascual O'Dogherty. 2003. *Foreign Banks Entry in Emerging Market Economies: A Host Country Perspective*. Mexico City: Banco de México.

Carkovic, Maria, and Ross Levine. 2005. Does Foreign Direct Investment Accelerate Economic Growth? In *Does Foreign Direct Investment Promote Development?* ed. Theodore Moran, Edward Graham, and Magnus Blomström. Washington: Peterson Institute for International Economics.

Chamon, Marcos, and Eswar Prasad. 2010. Why Are Saving Rates of Urban Households in China Rising? *American Economic Journal: Macroeconomics* 2, no. 1: 93–130.

Chari, Anusha, and Peter Henry. 2004. Risk Sharing and Asset Prices: Evidence from a Natural Experiment. *Journal of Finance* 59, no. 3 (June): 1295–324.

Chinn, Menzie, and Hiro Ito. 2006. What Matters for Financial Development? Capital Controls, Institutions, and Interactions. *Journal of Development Economics* 81, no. 1 (October): 163–92.

Chinn, Menzie, and Hiro Ito. 2008. A New Measure of Financial Openness. *Journal of Comparative Policy Analysis* 10, no. 3 (September): 309–22.

Claessens, Stijn, Asli Demirgüc-Kunt, and Harry Huizinga, H. 2001. How Does Foreign Entry Affect Domestic Banking Markets? *Journal of Banking and Finance* 25, no. 5 (May): 891–911.

Claessens, Stijn, Asli Demirgüc-Kunt, and Harry Huizinga. 2000. How Does Foreign Entry Affect the Domestic Banking Market? In *The Internationalization of Financial Services: Issues and Lessons for Developing Countries,* ed. Stijn Claessens and Marion Jansen. London: Kluwer Law International.

Clarke, George, Robert Cull, and Martinez Peria. 2001. *Does Foreign Bank Penetration Reduce Access to Credit in Developing Countries?* World Bank Policy Research Working Paper Series 2716 (September). Washington: World Bank.

Cline, William. 2010. *Financial Globalization, Economic Growth, and the Crisis of 2007–09.* Washington: Peterson Institute for International Economics.

Coase, Ronald. 2001. Quoted in Gordon Tullcok, A Comment on Daniel Klein's "A Plea to Economists Who Favor Liberty." *Eastern Economic Journal* (Spring), note 2.

Crystal, Jennifer, Gerard Dages, and Linda Goldberg. 2001. *Does Foreign Ownership Contribute to Sounder Banks in Emerging Markets? The Latin American Experience.* Federal Reserve Bank of New York Staff Report 137. New York: Federal Reserve Bank of New York.

De Gregorio, José, Sebastian Edwards, and Rodrigo Valdés. 2000. Controls on Capital Inflows: Do They Work? *Journal of Development Economics* 63, no. 1 (October): 59–83.

Desai, Mihir, Fritz Foley, and James Hines. 2006. Capital Controls, Liberalizations, and Foreign Direct Investment. *Review of Financial Studies* 19, no. 4 (Winter): 1433–64.

De Haas, Ralph, and Iman Van Lelyveld. 2006. Foreign Banks and Credit Stability in Central and Eastern Europe: A Panel Data Analysis. *Journal of Banking and Finance* 30, no. 7 (July): 1927–52.

Demirgüç-Kunt, Asli, and Harry Huizinga. 1999. Determinants of Commercial Bank Interest Margins and Profitability: Some International Evidence. *World Bank Economic Review* 13, no. 2: 379–408.

Demirgüç-Kunt, Asli, and Ross Levine. 2008. *Finance, Financial Sector Policies, and Long-Run Growth.* World Bank Policy Research Working Paper 4469 (January). Washington: World Bank.

Denizer, Cevdet. 2000. Foreign Entry in Turkey's Banking Sector, 1980–1997. In *The Internationalization of Financial Services: Issues and Lessons for Developing Countries,* ed. Stijn Claessens and Marion Jansen. London: Kluwer Law International.

Desai, Mihir A., C. Fritz Foley, and James R. Hines Jr. 2006. Capital Controls, Liberalizations, and Foreign Direct Investment. *Review of Financial Studies* 19, no. 4 (Winter): 1399–431.

Domanski, Dietrich. 2005. Foreign Banks in Emerging Market Economies: Changing Players, Changing Issues. *BIS Quarterly Review* (December). Basel: Bank for International Settlements.

Dornbusch, Rudiger. 1996. It's Time for a Financial Transactions Tax. *International Economics* (August/September): 95–96.

Dornbusch, Rudiger. 1998. Capital Controls: An Idea Whose Time Is Past. In *Should the IMF Pursue Capital-Account Convertibility?* Essays in International Finance no. 207 (May): 20–28. Princeton, NJ: International Finance Section, Department of Economics, Princeton University.

Edison, Hali, Ross Levine, Luca Ricci, and Torsten Slok. 2002. International Financial Integration and Economic Growth. *Journal of International Money and Finance* 21, no. 6 (November): 749–76.

Edwards, Sebastian. 1999. How Effective Are Capital Controls? *Journal of Economic Perspectives* 13, no. 4 (Fall): 65–84.

Edwards, Sebastian. 2001. *Capital Mobility and Economic Performance: Are Emerging Economies Different?* NBER Working Paper 8076 (January). Cambridge, MA: National Bureau of Economic Research

Eichengreen, Barry, Rachita Gullapalli, and Ugo Panizza. 2011. Capital Account Liberalization, Financial Development and Industry Growth: A Synthetic View. *Journal of International Money and Finance* 30, no. 6 (October): 1090–1106.

Eschenbach, Felix, Joseph F. Francois, and Ludger Schuknecht. 2000. Financial Sector Openness and Economic Growth. In *The Internationalization of Financial Services: Issues and Lessons for Developing Countries,* ed. Stijn Claessens and Marion Jansen. London: Kluwer Law International.

Fischer, Stanley. 2003. Globalization and Its Challenges. *American Economic Review* 93, no. 2 (May): 1–30.

Flood, Robert, and Peter Garber. 1984. Collapsing Exchange-Rate Regimes: Some Linear Examples. *Journal of International Economics* 17, no. 1-2 (August): 1–13.

Forbes, Kristin. 2005. Capital Controls: Mud in the Wheels of Market Efficiency. *Cato Journal* 25, no. 1: 153–66.

Forbes, Kristin. 2007a. The Microeconomic Evidence on Capital Controls: No Free Lunch. In *Capital Controls and Capital Flows in Emerging Economies: Policies, Practices and Consequences*, ed. Sebastian Edwards. Chicago: University of Chicago Press for NBER.

Forbes, Kristin. 2007b. One Cost of the Chilean Capital Controls: Increased Financial Constraints for Smaller Traded Firms. *Journal of International Economics* 71, no. 2: 294–323.

Friedman, Tom. 2000. *The Lexus and the Olive Tree.* New York: Anchor Books.

Gagnon, Joseph E., and Gary Clyde Hufbauer. 2011. Taxing China's Assets: How to Increase US Employment without Launching a Trade War. *Foreign Affairs* (April 25).

Gallego, Francisco, and Leonardo Hernández. 2003. Microeconomic Effects of Capital Controls: The Chilean Experience During the 1990s. *International Journal of Finance and Economics* 8, no. 3 (July): 225–53.

Gallego, Francisco, Leonardo Hernández, and Klaus Schmidt-Hebbel. 1999. *Capital Controls in Chile: Effective? Efficient?* Working Paper 59. Santiago: Central Bank of Chile.

Giannetti, Mariassunta, and Steven Ongena. 2009. Financial Integration and Firm Performance: Evidence from Foreign Bank Entry in Emerging Markets. *Review of Finance* 13, no. 2 (April): 181–223.

Goldberg, Linda. 2007. Financial Sector FDI and Host Countries: New and Old Lessons. *Economic Policy Review* 13, no. 1 (March). New York: Federal Reserve Bank of New York.

Goldsmith, Raymond. 1969. *Financial Structure and Development.* New Haven: Yale University Press.

Gourinchas, Pierre-Olivier, and Olivier Jeanne. 2007. *Capital Flows to Developing Countries: The Allocation Puzzle.* NBER Working Paper 13602 (November). Cambridge, MA: National Bureau of Economic Research.

Grilli, Vittorio. 1986. Buying and Selling Attacks on Fixed Exchange Rate Systems. *Journal of International Economics* 20, no. 1-2 (February): 143–56.

Grubel, Herbert. 1977. *International Economics.* Homewood, IL: Irwin.

Hanson, Samuel, Anil Kashyap, and Jeremy Stein. 2011. A Macroprudential Approach to Financial Regulation. *Journal of Economic Perspectives* 25, no. 1 (Winter): 3–28.

Hausmann, Ricardo, Lant Pritchett, and Dani Rodrik. 2005. Growth Accelerations. *Journal of Economic Growth* 10, no. 4: 303–29.

Henry, Peter. 2000a. Do Stock Market Liberalizations Cause Investment Booms? *Journal of Financial Economics* 58, no. 1-2 (September): 301–34.

Henry, Peter. 2000b. Stock Market Liberalization, Economic Reform, and Emerging Market Equity Prices. *Journal of Finance* 55, no. 2 (April): 529–64.

Henry, Peter. 2003. Capital-Account Liberalization, the Cost of Capital, and Economic Growth. *American Economic Review* 93, no. 2 (May): 91–96.

Henry, Peter. 2007. Capital Account Liberalization: Theory, Evidence, and Speculation. *Journal of Economic Literature* 45, no. 4 (December): 887–935.

IDB (Inter-American Development Bank). 2004. *Unlocking Credit: The Quest for Deep and Stable Bank Lending*. Washington.

IDB (Inter-American Development Bank). 2005. *Economic and Social Progress Report*. Washington.

IMF (International Monetary Fund). 2011. *Recent Experiences in Managing Capital Inflows—Cross-Cutting Themes and Possible Policy Framework*. Policy Paper. Washington. Available at www.imf.org/external/np/pp/eng/2011/021411a.pdf.

Javorcik, Beata. 2004. Does Foreign Direct Investment Increase the Productivity of Domestic Firms? In Search of Spillovers Through Backward Linkages. *American Economic Review* 94, no. 3: 605–27.

Javorcik, Beata, and Mariana Spatareanu. 2008. To Share or Not To Share: Does Local Participation Matter for Spillovers from Foreign Direct Investment? *Journal of Development Economics* 85, no. 1-2: 194–217.

Jeanne, Olivier. 2011. Capital Account Policies and the Real Exchange Rate. Baltimore, MD: Johns Hopkins University. Manuscript.

Jeanne, Olivier, and Anton Korinek. 2010a. Excessive Volatility in Capital Flows: A Pigouvian Taxation Approach. *American Economic Review Papers and Proceedings* 100, no. 2 (May): 403–07.

Jeanne, Olivier, and Anton Korinek. 2010b. *Managing Credit Booms and Busts: A Pigouvian Taxation Approach*. NBER Working Paper 16377 (September). Cambridge, MA: National Bureau of Economic Research.

Jeanne, Olivier, and Romain Rancière. 2011. The Optimal Level of International Reserves for Emerging Market Countries: A New Formula and Some Applications. *Economic Journal* 121, no. 555: 905–30.

Johnson, Simon, Kalpana Kochhar, Todd Mitton, and Natalia Tamirisa. 2007. Malaysian Capital Controls: Macroeconomics and Institutions. In *Capital Controls and Capital Flows in Emerging Economies: Policies, Practices and Consequences*, ed. Sebastian Edwards. Chicago: University of Chicago Press for National Bureau of Economic Research.

Johnson, Simon, William Larson, Chris Papageorgiou, and Arvind Subramanian. 2009. *Is Newer Better? Penn World Table Revisions and Their Impact on Growth Estimates*. NBER Working Paper no. 15455. Cambridge, MA: National Bureau of Economic Research (October).

Johnson, Simon, Jonathan Ostry, and Arvind, Subramanian. 2010. Prospects for Sustained Growth in Africa: Benchmarking the Constraints. *IMF Staff Papers* 57, no. 1: 119–71.

Kaplan, Ethan, and Dani Rodrik. 2002. Did the Malaysian Capital Controls Work? In *Preventing Currency Crises in Emerging Markets*, ed. Sebastian Edwards and Jeffrey Frankel. Chicago: University of Chicago Press for National Bureau of Economic Research.

Keynes, John Maynard. 1933. National Self-Sufficiency. *The Yale Review* 22, no. 4 (June): 755–69.

Keynes, John Maynard. 1936. *The General Theory of Employment, Interest and Money*. New York: Harcourt Brace and Co.

Kim, Woochan, and Shang-Jin Wei. 2002. Offshore Investment Funds: Monsters in Emerging Markets? *Journal of Development Economics* 68, no. 1 (June): 205–24.

Klein, Michael. 2005. *Capital Account Liberalization, Institutional Quality and Economic Growth: Theory and Evidence*. NBER Working Paper 11112 (February). Cambridge, MA: National Bureau of Economic Research.

Korinek, Anton. 2010. *Regulating Capital Flows to Emerging Markets: An Externality View*. College Park, MD: University of Maryland. Unpublished manuscript.

Korinek, Anton. 2011. The New Economics of Prudential Capital Controls: A Research Agenda. *IMF Economic Review* 59, no. 3 (August): 524–61.

Kose, Ayhan, Eswar Prasad, Kenneth Rogoff, and Shang-Jin Wei. 2009. Financial Globalization: A Reappraisal. *IMF Staff Papers* 56, no. 1 (April): 8–62.

Kose, Ayhan, Eswar Prasad, and Marco Terrones. 2009. Does Openness to International Financial Flows Raise Productivity Growth? *Journal of International Money and Finance* 28, no. 4 (June): 554–80.

Krugman, Paul. 1979. A Model of Balance-of-Payments Crises. *Journal of Money, Credit and Banking* 11, no. 3 (August): 311–25.

Lane, Philip, and Gian Maria Milesi-Ferretti. 2007. The External Wealth of Nations Mark II: Revised and Extended Estimates of Foreign Assets and Liabilities, 1970–2004. *Journal of International Economics* 73, no. 2 (November): 223–50.

Lardy, Nicholas, and Patrick Douglass. 2011. *Capital Account Liberalization and the Role of the Renminbi.* Working Paper 11-6 (February). Washington: Peterson Institute for International Economics.

Le Fort, Guillermo, and Sergio Lehmann. 2000. El Encaje, Los Flujos de Capitales y el Gasto: Una Evaluación Empírica. *Documentos de Trabajo*, no. 64. Santiago: Central Bank of Chile.

Levine, Ross. 1997. Financial Development and Economic Growth: Views and Agenda. *Journal of Economic Literature* 35, no. 2 (June): 688–726.

Levine, Ross, and Sara Zervos. 1998. Capital Control Liberalization and Stock Market Development. *World Development* 26, no. 7 (July): 1169–83.

Lipsey, Robert. 2004. Home- and Host-Country Effects of Foreign Direct Investment. In *Challenges to Globalization: Analyzing the Economics*, ed. Robert Baldwin and Alan Winters. Chicago: University of Chicago Press for National Bureau of Economic Research.

Lipsey, Robert, and Fredrik Sjöholm. 2002. *Foreign Firms and Indonesian Manufacturing Wages: An Analysis with Panel Data.* NBER Working Paper 9417 (December). Cambridge, MA: National Bureau of Economic Research.

Magud, Nicolas, Carmen Reinhart, and Kenneth Rogoff. 2011. *Capital Controls: Myth and Reality: A Portfolio Balance Approach to Capital Controls.* Working Paper 11-7. Washington: Peterson Institute for International Economics.

Mathieson, Donald J., and Jorge Roldós. 2001. Foreign Banks and Emerging Markets. In *Open Doors: Foreign Participation in Financial Systems in Developing Countries*, ed. Robert Litan, Paul Masson, and Michael Pomerleano. Washington: Brookings Institution.

Mattoo, Aaditya, and Arvind Subramanian. 2008. *Currency Undervaluation and Sovereign Wealth Funds: A New Role for the World Trade Organization.* Working Paper 08-2 (January). Washington: Peterson Institute for International Economics.

McKinnon, Ronald. 1973. *Money and Capital in Economic Development.* Washington: Brookings Institution.

Messerlin, Patrick. 2004. China in the WTO: Antidumping and Safeguards. In *China and the WTO: Accession, Policy Reform, and Poverty Reduction Strategies*, ed. Deepak Bhattasali, Shantong Li, and Will Martin. Washington: World Bank and Oxford University Press.

Mian, Atif. 2003. *Foreign, Private Domestic and Government Banks: New Evidence from Emerging Markets.* Chicago: University of Chicago Graduate School of Business. Unpublished manuscript.

Micco, Alejandro, Ugo Panizza, and Mónica Yañez. 2004. *Bank Ownership and Performance.* IDB Working Paper 518. Washington: Inter-American Development Bank (November).

Milesi-Ferretti, Gian Maria, and Cedric Tille. 2011. The Great Retrenchment: International Capital Flows During the Global Financial Crisis. *Economic Policy* 26, no. 66 (April): 285–342.

Mishkin, Frederic. 2006. *The Next Great Globalization: How Disadvantaged Nations Can Harness Their Financial Systems to Get Rich.* Princeton, NJ: Princeton University Press.

Mitton, Todd. 2006. Stock Market Liberalization and Operating Performance at the Firm Level. *Journal of Financial Economics* 81, no. 3 (September): 625–47.

Moran, Theodore. 2002. *Beyond Sweatshops: Foreign Direct Investment and Globalization in Developing Countries*. Washington: Brookings Institution.

Moran, Theodore, Edward Graham, and Magnus Blomström. 2005. *Does Foreign Direct Investment Promote Development?* Washington: Peterson Institute for International Economics.

Moreno, Ramon, and Agustin Villar. 2005. *The Increased Role of Foreign Bank Entry in Emerging Markets*. BIS Paper 23 (May). Basel: Bank for International Settlements.

Obstfeld, Maurice. 1996. Models of Currency Crises with Self-fulfilling Features. *European Economic Review* 40, no. 3-5: 1037–47.

Obstfeld, Maurice. 2009. International Finance and Growth in Developing Countries: What Have We Learned? *IMF Staff Papers* 56, no. 1 (March).

Ostry, Jonathan D., Atish Ghosh, Karl Habermeier, Marcos Chamon, Mahvash Qureshi, and Dennis Reinhardt. 2010. *Capital Inflows: The Role of Controls*. IMF Staff Position Note 10/04. Washington: International Monetary Fund.

Ostry, Jonathan D., Atish R. Ghosh, Karl Habermeier, Luc Laeven, Marcos Chamon, Mahvash S. Qureshi, and Annamaria Kokenyne. 2011. *Managing Capital Inflows: What Tools to Use?* IMF Staff Discussion Note 11/06. Washington: International Monetary Fund.

Parikh, Kirit. 1997. *India Development Report*. New Delhi: Oxford University Press.

Pomerleano, Michael, and George J. Vojta. 2001. Foreign Banks and Emerging Markets: An Institutional Study. In *Open Doors: Foreign Participation in Financial Systems in Developing Countries,* ed. Robert Litan, Paul Masson, and Michael Pomerleano. Washington: Brookings Institution.

Prasad, Eswar, Raghuram Rajan, and Arvind Subramanian. 2007. Foreign Capital and Economic Growth. *Brookings Papers on Economic Activity* 38, no. 1: 153–230.

Prasad, Eswar, and Shang-Jin Wei. 2007. The Chinese Approach to Capital Inflows: Patterns and Possible Explanations. In *Capital Controls and Capital Flows in Emerging Economies: Policies, Practices, and Consequences,* ed. Sebastian Edwards. Chicago: University of Chicago Press for National Bureau of Economic Research.

Quinn, Dennis, and Maria Toyoda. 2008. Does Capital Account Liberalization Lead to Growth? *Review of Financial Studies* 21, no. 3 (November): 1403–49.

Rajan, Raghuram, and Luigi Zingales. 1998. Financial Dependence and Growth. *American Economic Review* 88, no. 3 (June): 559–86.

Rhee, Yung Whee, and Therese Belot. 1990. *Export Catalysts in Low-Income Countries: A Review of Eleven Success Stories*. World Bank Discussion Paper 72 (July). Washington: World Bank.

Rodrik, Dani. 1998. Who Needs Capital-Account Convertibility? *Essays in International Finance*. Princeton, NJ: Princeton University (February).

Rodrik, Dani. 2008. The Real Exchange Rate and Economic Growth. *Brookings Papers on Economic Activity* 2008, no. 2: 365–412.

Rodrik, Dani. 2010. Making Room for China in the World Economy. *American Economic Review, Papers & Proceedings* 100, no. 2 (May): 89–91.

Rodrik, Dani, and Arvind Subramanian. 2009. Why Did Financial Globalization Disappoint? *IMF Staff Papers* 56, no. 1: 112–38.

Roodman, David. 2008. *A Note on the Theme of Too Many Instruments*. Working Paper 125 (May). Washington: Center for Global Development.

Rothenberg, Alexander D., and Francis Warnock. 2006. *Sudden Flight and True Sudden Stops*. NBER Working Paper 12726. Cambridge, MA: National Bureau of Economic Research.

Sala-i-Martin, Xavier. 1997. I Just Ran Two Million Regressions. *American Economic Review* 87, no. 2 (May): 178–83.

Sala-i-Martin, Xavier, Gernot Doppelhofer, and Ronald Miller. 2004. Determinants of Long-Term Growth: A Bayesian Averaging of Classical Estimates (BACE) Approach. *American Economic Review* 94, no. 4 (September): 813–35.

Schindler, Martin. 2009. Measuring Financial Integration: A New Data Set. *IMF Staff Papers* 56, no. 1: 222–38.

Song, Zheng, Kjetil Storesletten, and Fabrizio Zilibotti. 2011. Growing Like China. *American Economic Review* 101, no. 1: 196–233.

Strauss-Kahn, Dominique. 2011. Opening remarks at a lecture and discussion on "Towards a More Stable International Monetary System," International Monetary Fund, February 10, Washington.

Tytell, Irina, and Shang-Jin Wei. 2004. *Does Financial Globalization Induce Better Macroeconomic Policies?* IMF Working Paper 04/84 (May). Washington: International Monetary Fund.

Williamson, John. 1990. What Washington Means by Policy Reform. In *Latin American Adjustment: How Much Has Happened?* ed. John Williamson. Washington: Institute for International Economics.

Williamson, John. 2000. *Exchange Rate Regimes for Emerging Markets: Reviving the Intermediate Option.* Washington: Institute for International Economics.

Zee, Howell. 1999. *Retarding Short-Term Capital Inflows Through a Withholding Tax.* IMF Working Paper 00/40 (March). Washington: International Monetary Fund.

Index

Other Publications from the Peterson Institute for International Economics

T. N. Srinivasan and Suresh D. Tendulkar
March 2003   ISBN 0-88132-280-6
After the Washington Consensus: Restarting Growth and Reform in Latin America
Pedro-Pablo Kuczynski and John Williamson, eds.
March 2003   ISBN 0-88132-347-0
The Decline of US Labor Unions and the Role of Trade   Robert E. Baldwin
June 2003   ISBN 0-88132-341-1
Can Labor Standards Improve under Globalization?   Kimberly Ann Elliott and Richard B. Freeman
June 2003   ISBN 0-88132-332-2
Crimes and Punishments? Retaliation under the WTO   Robert Z. Lawrence
October 2003   ISBN 0-88132-359-4
Inflation Targeting in the World Economy
Edwin M. Truman
October 2003   ISBN 0-88132-345-4
Foreign Direct Investment and Tax Competition   John H. Mutti
November 2003   ISBN 0-88132-352-7
Has Globalization Gone Far Enough? The Costs of Fragmented Markets
Scott C. Bradford and Robert Z. Lawrence
February 2004   ISBN 0-88132-349-7
Food Regulation and Trade: Toward a Safe and Open Global System   Tim Josling, Donna Roberts, and David Orden
March 2004   ISBN 0-88132-346-2
Controlling Currency Mismatches in Emerging Markets   Morris Goldstein and Philip Turner
April 2004   ISBN 0-88132-360-8
Free Trade Agreements: US Strategies and Priorities   Jeffrey J. Schott, ed.
April 2004   ISBN 0-88132-361-6
Trade Policy and Global Poverty
William R. Cline
June 2004   ISBN 0-88132-365-9
Bailouts or Bail-ins? Responding to Financial Crises in Emerging Economies
Nouriel Roubini and Brad Setser
August 2004   ISBN 0-88132-371-3
Transforming the European Economy
Martin Neil Baily and Jacob Funk Kirkegaard
September 2004   ISBN 0-88132-343-8
Chasing Dirty Money: The Fight Against Money Laundering   Peter Reuter and Edwin M. Truman
November 2004   ISBN 0-88132-370-5
The United States and the World Economy: Foreign Economic Policy for the Next Decade
C. Fred Bergsten
January 2005   ISBN 0-88132-380-2
Does Foreign Direct Investment Promote Development?   Theodore H. Moran, Edward M. Graham, and Magnus Blomström, eds.
April 2005   ISBN 0-88132-381-0
American Trade Politics, 4th ed.   I. M. Destler
June 2005   ISBN 0-88132-382-9

Why Does Immigration Divide America? Public Finance and Political Opposition to Open Borders   Gordon H. Hanson
August 2005   ISBN 0-88132-400-0
Reforming the US Corporate Tax
Gary Clyde Hufbauer and Paul L. E. Grieco
September 2005   ISBN 0-88132-384-5
The United States as a Debtor Nation
William R. Cline
September 2005   ISBN 0-88132-399-3
NAFTA Revisited: Achievements and Challenges   Gary Clyde Hufbauer and Jeffrey J. Schott, assisted by Paul L. E. Grieco and Yee Wong
October 2005   ISBN 0-88132-334-9
US National Security and Foreign Direct Investment   Edward M. Graham and David M. Marchick
May 2006   ISBN 978-0-88132-391-7
Accelerating the Globalization of America: The Role for Information Technology
Catherine L. Mann, assisted by Jacob Funk Kirkegaard
June 2006   ISBN 978-0-88132-390-0
Delivering on Doha: Farm Trade and the Poor
Kimberly Ann Elliott
July 2006   ISBN 978-0-88132-392-4
Case Studies in US Trade Negotiation, Vol. 1: Making the Rules   Charan Devereaux, Robert Z. Lawrence, and Michael Watkins
September 2006   ISBN 978-0-88132-362-7
Case Studies in US Trade Negotiation, Vol. 2: Resolving Disputes   Charan Devereaux, Robert Z. Lawrence, and Michael Watkins
September 2006   ISBN 978-0-88132-363-2
C. Fred Bergsten and the World Economy
Michael Mussa, ed.
December 2006   ISBN 978-0-88132-397-9
Working Papers, Volume I   Peterson Institute
December 2006   ISBN 978-0-88132-388-7
The Arab Economies in a Changing World
Marcus Noland and Howard Pack
April 2007   ISBN 978-0-88132-393-1
Working Papers, Volume II   Peterson Institute
April 2007   ISBN 978-0-88132-404-4
Global Warming and Agriculture: Impact Estimates by Country   William R. Cline
July 2007   ISBN 978-0-88132-403-7
US Taxation of Foreign Income
Gary Clyde Hufbauer and Ariel Assa
October 2007   ISBN 978-0-88132-405-1
Russia's Capitalist Revolution: Why Market Reform Succeeded and Democracy Failed
Anders Åslund
October 2007   ISBN 978-0-88132-409-9
Economic Sanctions Reconsidered, 3d ed.
Gary Clyde Hufbauer, Jeffrey J. Schott, Kimberly Ann Elliott, and Barbara Oegg
November 2007
                    ISBN hardcover 978-0-88132-407-5
    ISBN hardcover/CD-ROM 978-0-88132-408-2

WORKS IN PROGRESS

DISTRIBUTORS OUTSIDE THE UNITED STATES

**Australia, New Zealand,
and Papua New Guinea**
D. A. Information Services
648 Whitehorse Road
Mitcham, Victoria 3132, Australia
Tel: 61-3-9210-7777
Fax: 61-3-9210-7788
Email: service@dadirect.com.au
www.dadirect.com.au

India, Bangladesh, Nepal, and Sri Lanka
Viva Books Private Limited
Mr. Vinod Vasishtha
4737/23 Ansari Road
Daryaganj, New Delhi 110002
India
Tel: 91-11-4224-2200
Fax: 91-11-4224-2240
Email: viva@vivagroupindia.net
www.vivagroupindia.com

**Mexico, Central America, South America,
and Puerto Rico**
US PubRep, Inc.
311 Dean Drive
Rockville, MD 20851
Tel: 301-838-9276
Fax: 301-838-9278
Email: c.falk@ieee.org

Asia (*Brunei, Burma, Cambodia, China,
Hong Kong, Indonesia, Korea, Laos, Malaysia,
Philippines, Singapore, Taiwan, Thailand,
and Vietnam*)
East-West Export Books (EWEB)
University of Hawaii Press
2840 Kolowalu Street
Honolulu, Hawaii 96822-1888
Tel: 808-956-8830
Fax: 808-988-6052
Email: eweb@hawaii.edu

Canada
Renouf Bookstore
5369 Canotek Road, Unit 1
Ottawa, Ontario KlJ 9J3, Canada
Tel: 613-745-2665
Fax: 613-745-7660
www.renoufbooks.com

Japan
United Publishers Services Ltd.
1-32-5, Higashi-shinagawa
Shinagawa-ku, Tokyo 140-0002
Japan
Tel: 81-3-5479-7251
Fax: 81-3-5479-7307
Email: purchasing@ups.co.jp
*For trade accounts only. Individuals will find
Institute books in leading Tokyo bookstores.*

Middle East
MERIC
2 Bahgat Ali Street, El Masry Towers
Tower D, Apt. 24
Zamalek, Cairo
Egypt
Tel. 20-2-7633824
Fax: 20-2-7369355
Email: mahmoud_fouda@mericonline.com
www.mericonline.com

United Kingdom, Europe
(*including Russia and Turkey*)**, Africa,
and Israel**
The Eurospan Group
c/o Turpin Distribution
Pegasus Drive
Stratton Business Park
Biggleswade, Bedfordshire
SG18 8TQ
United Kingdom
Tel: 44 (0) 1767-604972
Fax: 44 (0) 1767-601640
Email: eurospan@turpin-distribution.com
www.eurospangroup.com/bookstore

**Visit our website at:
www.piie.com
E-mail orders to:
petersonmail@presswarehouse.com**